The Land of Doing Without

Davey Gunn of the Hollyford

Other books by Julia Bradshaw:

Miners in the Clouds: A hundred years of scheelite mining at Glenorchy
(Lakes District Museum, 1997)

The Far Downers: The people and history of Haast and Jackson Bay
(Otago University Press, 2001)

Arrowtown History and Walks (Otago University Press, 2001)

The Land of Doing Without

Davey Gunn of the Hollyford

JULIA BRADSHAW

CANTERBURY UNIVERSITY PRESS

UNIVERSITY OF
CANTERBURY
Te Whare Wānanga o Waitaha
CHRISTCHURCH NEW ZEALAND

First published in 2007 by
CANTERBURY UNIVERSITY PRESS
University of Canterbury
Private Bag 4800
Christchurch
NEW ZEALAND

www.cup.canterbury.ac.nz

ISBN 978-1-877257-53-7

A catalogue record for this book is available from
the National Library of New Zealand

Reprinted 2007, 2008, 2015

Editing, design and pre-press production by Rachel Scott

Printed by Caxton, New Zealand

Cover: A hand-coloured photograph by Elsie K. Morton
of Davey Gunn at Martins Bay.
Murray Gunn Collection

Half-title page: Davey with Bess, a favourite dog, in 1951.
Derek and Pat Turnbull Collection

Contents

For Murray Gunn,
who lived in the
Hollyford Valley for 50 years

Acknowledgements

Thanks first to Murray Gunn, who suggested the project but made it clear that I was free to write whatever I chose. Murray gave me unlimited access to his collection of material about his father and the Hollyford, and was extremely good at identifying photographs, suggesting who to contact and answering questions. Murray's sisters, Isabel Findlay and Dorothy Parlane, were also supportive and provided additional information and photographs.

The quotes and anecdotes within this book add an enormous amount of life to it and I am very grateful to Ed Cotter, Alan De La Mare, Jean Greenslade, Arnold Grey, Doug Gunn, Ian Haggitt, Daphne Midgley, Jean Prust, Alan Snook, Derek Turnbull, Brian and Ruth Waddell and Eoin Wylie for sharing their memories. Thank you to Morag Forrester, Geoff Spearpoint, Jennifer Beveridge and Sound Archives Nga Taonga Korero for permission to quote from other interviews.

Such was the respect for Davey that his friends, the children of his friends, his former workers and even people who had met him only once – or occasionally not at all – were eager to assist, and their enthusiasm for the project was a great motivator for me. Special thanks are due to Ian Speden for his generosity with his time and especially for collecting me from the train station, and to Pat and the late Derek Turnbull, who travelled to the Hollyford especially to talk to me.

Thanks are due also to the following people who supplied information and photographs: Dorothy Andrews, Mike Bennett, Lesley Board, Allan Boyer, Bill Brown, David Clarke, Ed Cotter, Tony Gates, Ann Irving, Garth King, Graham Langton, Peter Marshall, Elfin McDonald, Robin McNeil, Ian Robertson, Peter Robson, Betty Shaw, Rata Sibley, Kathleen Stringer, Brian Swete, Mary Thomson, Paula White and

Freeman Willetts. I am grateful to Albert Downing for copying old photos.

The staff of the following institutions were, as always, very helpful: Archives New Zealand/Te Rua Mahara o te Kawanatanga (Wellington, Dunedin and Christchurch offices), the Alexander Turnbull Library, the Waimate District and Historical Society, the North Otago Museum, the Hocken Library, the Alexandra Museum, the Lakes District Museum, the Middlemarch Museum and Invercargill City Libraries.

Thanks to Rachel Scott for being such a cheerful editor, and to Richard King and Kaye Godfrey at Canterbury University Press.

For permission to reproduce material I am grateful to Thelma Bradshaw, Robyn Matheson, Brian Swete, Dusty Spittle, Sylvia Morris, Jack Sowery, Reed Publishing (NZ) Ltd, the Hocken Library and Archives New Zealand.

Many thanks to Megan Anderson, Aaron Braden and Eddie Newman for their comments on the manuscript, to Erik Bradshaw and Christine Ryan for computer support, and to Margaret and John Bradshaw for trying to do something about the garden. Thanks to Neil Drysdale, Russell Baker and all those who provided accommodation and company at Martins Bay and Big Bay during my visits. Thanks also to Hollyford Valley Walk for flying food (and, most important, wine) into Martins Bay.

Preface

I first heard about Davey Gunn when I started working as a track guide for the Hollyford Valley Tourist Company Ltd in 1990, and began reading everything I could find about Martins Bay and the Hollyford Valley.

I soon realised that Davey Gunn had been a remarkable character. He was a heroic figure who had made an amazing 20-hour journey on foot from Big Bay to the Milford Road to get assistance for people injured in a plane crash. In an area known for its ruggedness and isolation, Davey relished the challenge of wrestling with feisty wild cattle. He was a visionary who appreciated the beauty of the Hollyford Valley and organised guided trips so that others could enjoy it too.

I was captivated by the Hollyford myself, and, walking over much of Davey's country (and spending numerous days in the Fiordland rain), I began to wonder just what kind of character could have survived there for nearly 30 years.

What was he doing there in the first place? He had not been lured by fantastic government promises like the early settlers: Davey Gunn arrived when the area had well and truly been given up on. How did he make any money out of the place and, if he wasn't making a living, why did he stay? How did he survive so many years of living virtually alone, separated from the rest of his family?

Davey's son, Murray, began to fill out the picture for me, but it took numerous interviews and discussions with many others before I felt I was beginning to discover the man behind the legend. Davey Gunn is still one of my heroes, though now with all the foibles that make someone human.

It was Davey who called the Hollyford 'the land of doing without', because it didn't have any 'modern inconveniences'. New-fangled machinery exasperated him, and modern facilities were expensive – he was pleased and proud that he could manage without.

He was known to his friends as Dave or Davey, but hardly ever as David. Of the various possible spellings I have chosen to use Davey, as this is the form used on his memorial plaque at Lower Pyke, where he is referred to as 'Davey the trampers friend'.

Julia Bradshaw
Hokitika, 2007

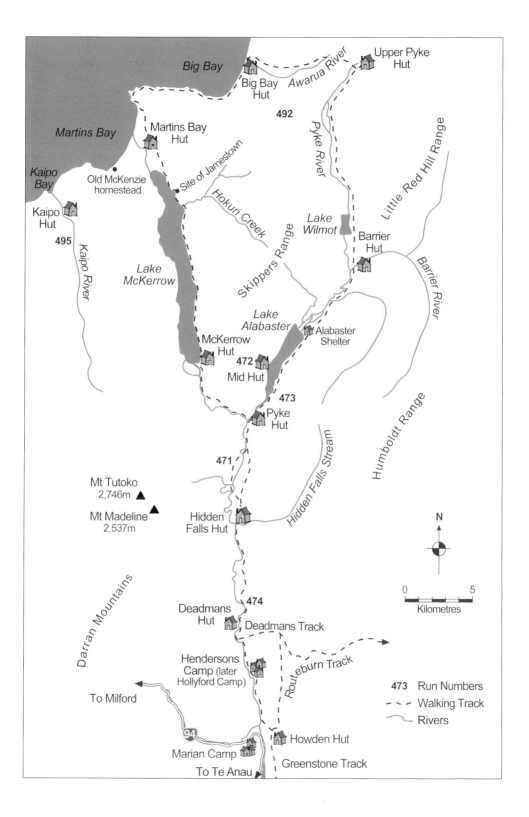

Big Bay

Martins Bay

Kaipo
Bay

Kaipo
Hut
495

Martins Bay
Hut

Old McKenzie
homestead

Site of Jamestown

Kaipo River

Lake
McKerrow

Hokuri Creek

Skippers Range

Big Bay
Hut

492

Awarua River

Pyke River

Upper Pyke
Hut

Little Red Hill Range

Lake
Wilmot

Barrier
Hut

Barrier River

McKerrow
Hut

Lake
Alabaster

Alabaster
Shelter

472

Mid Hut

473

Pyke
Hut

471

Mt Tutoko
2,746m ▲

Mt Madeline
2,537m ▲

Hidden Falls Stream

Humboldt Range

Hidden
Falls Hut

Darran Mountains

Deadmans
Hut

474

Deadmans Track

Hendersons
Camp (later
Hollyford Camp)

Routeburn Track

N

0   5
Kilometres

To Milford

94

Marian Camp

Howden Hut

Greenstone Track

To Te Anau

473   Run Numbers
- - -   Walking Track
——   Rivers

11

The Ballad of David John Gunn

Brian Swete

Been a lot of loose talk
About Davie Gunn,
working his cattle
on the Hollyford run.

But the coloured-up stories
and myths are quite wrong,
he was just another battler
struggling along.

Clearing the scrub,
swinging the axe.
Doing his best
to pay mortgage and tax.

His Hereford stock
were hounded through bogs,
mustered and driven
by half-wild dogs.

But they fattened up quick
on the long drive.
Bush-bred store cattle
soon learned to thrive.

Unwanted horses
were sent down to Dave.
Those that survived
soon learned to behave.

Worn out old harness
cobbled with rivets and wire.
Cast off shoes
refitted with fire.

The fording horse stumbled
and the girth broke,
drowning Dave Gunn
who could not swim a stroke.

Rushing white water
took him away,
and now the myth-makers
all want their say.

Now I worked with old Dave
back in the past,
and he knew the river
would get him at last.

So cut out the bullshit,
the legends and lies.
The heroic talk
that Dave would despise.

Let's just remember
the power of the man.
His years of survival
where wild rivers ran.

Chapter One

First Year in the Hollyford

One of the most daunting and formidable farming ventures ever undertaken in this country.[1]

When Davey Gunn rode his horse over the Greenstone Saddle on 22 August 1926 and began to descend the steep track to the Hollyford Valley, he scarcely imagined that he would spend the rest of his life devoted to the spectacular country unfolding before him. Little in his background had prepared him for this kind of rugged landscape. Born on a sheep station in the Waitaki Valley in 1887, Davey had been brought up on the vast tussock-covered sheep stations of Central Otago. He was the son of a Scottish shepherd who had risen through the ranks to the position of manager on Galloway Station, a large sheep run near Alexandra.[2] By contrast, the Hollyford was wet, forest-covered cattle country – wild-cattle country.

Alexander Gunn, Davey's father, about 1890, a few years after Davey's birth.
Alexandra Museum

However, Davey had several attributes that would be essential in the Hollyford: he was good with animals – especially dogs, he was an excellent horseman, was extremely tough, and took any disaster in his stride. After leaving school he had worked briefly as a clerk for a stock and station agency before deciding a desk job didn't suit him. He returned to the sheep farm owned by his Aunts Mary and Jessie, near Waimate, where he stayed until he was called up near the end of World War One. He only made it as far as Trentham Barracks before peace was declared, upon which he was discharged and returned to Waimate and married Ethel Willetts, a red-haired confectioner who enjoyed tennis and dancing.[3]

After their marriage the couple bought the lease to a 1,474-acre farm near Sutton, where they experienced the economic

Davey's mother, Isabella Gunn, at Galloway homestead, Alexandra, about 1913.

Doug Gunn

ups and downs associated with the postwar years. The rocky, tussock-covered terrain was tricky to farm. Irregular rainfall meant it was difficult to grow enough feed for winter, so stocking had to be light. Even during good years the farm provided only a modest income.[4]

The years after World War One were not a good time to be a farmer. During 1920–21 there was a slump that 'came with all the suddenness of a summer thunderstorm'. Land halved in value and 'stock prices tumbled like a stream running over a cliff'.[5] During the slump Davey struggled to maintain his sheep numbers, and when prices showed some improvement during 1925 he was determined to take advantage of them. In spring he bought lambs for 10 shillings each, with the idea of fattening them up on rape and turnips. He got a good price for the first load he sent away, but then the price dropped and he sold the remaining lambs at five shillings each.[6]

It was about this time that a friend of Davey's came to see him. This was probably either Patrick Fraser (from the near-

Davey as a boy, with his sisters, Gus (Sarah Augusta, left) and Jean.

Murray Gunn Collection

The Gunn family homestead at Hook Bush, Waimate. From left: Gordon Gunn (Davey's uncle), Mary Gunn (aunt), Jane Gunn (grand-mother), Jessie Gunn (aunt) and Mrs Goldsmith (a visitor).

Waimate District and Historical Society Archives

by town of Outram) or James Roberts (the son of a wealthy neighbour). He had with him a handful of photographs of several runs at Martins Bay in Fiordland.[7]

The Martins Bay runs consisted of six bush-covered cattle grazing leases in the Hollyford Valley and at Martins Bay, Big Bay and the Kaipo River.[8] The runs were extremely remote, even by contemporary standards, and long cattle drives were necessary to get stock to market. To Davey, plagued at Sutton by lack of rainfall, the photographs of Fiordland's lush forests and rivers would have been appealing. Not only did the country look attractive, but the proposition was a 'great spec', his friend assured him.[9] Davey was certainly interested. He liked a bit of adventure, and being a cowboy on the wild West Coast sounded exciting.

By this time Davey and Ethel had three children: Isabel (born in March 1920), Dorothy (born in January 1925) and Murray, who was only six months old when his father decided in mid-1926 to sell the farm and move to the Hollyford Valley. No one knows exactly why Davey ended up making the move

Ethel Willetts at about the time she married Davey, in 1919.

Murray Gunn Collection

without his family. According to his daughter Isabel, Davey initially assumed the family would accompany him to Martins Bay. When it was pointed out that the children needed to be educated, he suggested they live in Queenstown, which was the nearest large town. But it was unlikely the family could afford a house in Queenstown after Davey had paid his share for the Hollyford leases. Was Davey trying to escape from his marriage and family life? The marriage might have been under some strain, with Ethel feeling the effects of their isolation, and of having given birth to two children within a year. Ethel apparently never forgave Davey for selling the Sutton property just when she felt they were starting to get on their feet.[10]

In the event, Ethel was persuaded by her sister, Tilly Willetts, to go and live with her in Oamaru. Tilly ran Willetts Tea Rooms, a successful business that employed up to 23 people, and she was keen for Ethel to be her housekeeper. Ethel had friends and relations in the Oamaru/Waimate area, and no doubt the social life would have been an attractive proposition after her rather lonely existence at Sutton.[11]

On 28 June 1926 Davey and Patrick Fraser were in Dunedin signing the documents to acquire the pastoral leases previously owned by brothers Hugh and Malcolm McKenzie. They paid £50 to Hugh for the year-to-year grazing licences at Big Bay and Upper Pyke (Run 492, 16,900 acres) and the Kaipo River (Run 495, 1,500 acres), which had an annual rental of £10 each. Malcolm received £10 for his year-to-year grazing licence for 2,000 acres in the Deadmans/Hidden Falls area (annual rental

A view of the homestead near Sutton in the late 1930s.

Peter Marshall

Davey on the verandah of the homestead near Sutton in 1926, shortly before the family left the farm. With their father are Dorothy (left) and Isabel.

Murray Gunn Collection

£1).[12] A couple of weeks later, Malcolm McKenzie sold the pair (for an unknown sum) his grazing licence for Runs 471–474 (25,660 acres in the Hollyford Valley and Lower Pyke), which was due for renewal in three years' time.[13]

In August 1926, with the paperwork completed, Davey and Patrick Fraser began their great adventure. Ethel and the children had already left for Oamaru when Davey set off with his horses and dogs to the area that was to become the love of his life, Martins Bay and the Hollyford Valley.[14]

So, what kind of country did Davey disappear into? The Hollyford was isolated, often wet but very beautiful. A failed attempt during the 1870s at creating a link from Otago to Melbourne via a town and port at Martins Bay meant the area was moderately well known. Situated at the northern end of the almost impossibly rugged country of Fiordland and south of the slightly more benign landscape of South Westland, Martins Bay has a fascinating history. Even with today's modern technology and transport, it has escaped permanent settlement and is only home to visiting whitebaiters and the owners of a few baches.

Maori resident in South Westland utilised the lagoons and beaches of Martins Bay and neighbouring Big Bay, with archaeological remains having been found at both places. Early European visitors met a Ngai Tahu family – Tutoko, his wife and two daughters – who were living at Martins Bay during the 1860s but who later moved further north.[15]

It was during the 1860s, when Otago was in the grip of the

gold rush, that the idea of a western port linking Otago to Australia had first been suggested. Although initial reports on the prospects of a road from Queenstown to Martins Bay were unfavourable, the idea caught the imagination of the Superintendent of Otago, James Macandrew. By 1870 the town of Jamestown, on the shore of Lake McKerrow, was being surveyed and settlers were encouraged to go to Martins Bay. Unfortunately, the difficulties of using the Hollyford River mouth as a port had been greatly underestimated. In January 1870 the *Charles Edward*, carrying surveyors to Martins Bay, ran aground in the lower reaches of the river, and the *Esther Ann*, bringing in the first load of settlers, was wrecked on the bar six months later. Shipowners became reluctant to enter the river and, when the promised road failed to proceed, the settlement was doomed. Although the settlers were keen, the isolation and near starvation caused by the failure of stores to arrive caused the population to diminish from more than 50 settlers in 1871 to fewer than 10 in the late 1890s.[16]

The settlers who remained turned from cropping to larger-scale farming, taking up 50-acre blocks and running cattle or sheep. However, their isolation continued to make it difficult to earn a living. Any produce had, somehow, to be transported to the nearest market. Wool could be shipped, but live produce such as cattle had to be driven along bush tracks to Lake Wakatipu and then on to Queenstown.

In 1901 Daniel and Margaret McKenzie, who had settled in the area in the late 1870s, took up Runs 471–474, which consisted of 25,660 acres in the Hollyford Valley. Their son, Hugh McKenzie, leased Run 495 in the lower Kaipo Valley in March 1903, and Edward Henry (Ted) Green, from South Westland, took up Run 492 (16,900 acres at Big Bay) at about the same time. All periodically took cattle out to Lake Wakatipu. In 1910 Green took 30 head of cattle from Big Bay to Queenstown in 13 days – quite a feat. Another settler, John George, who kept sheep on his land at Martins Bay, would cart sacks of wool to the boat landing at the south side of the bay, where they were collected by men from the government supply ship *Hinemoa* when it was landing goods for the settlers.[17]

Daniel and Margaret McKenzie left Martins Bay about 1903, retiring to Glenorchy. Another son, Malcolm, took over the runs in the Hollyford, and Hugh McKenzie added to his area by taking over Ted Green's lease when Green gave up the run in 1919.[18]

Between them the McKenzie brothers now had leases covering about 45,000 acres, but less than 1,000 acres was open country. The balance was mostly either wetlands, land heavily covered with forest, or steep, bush-clad mountain slopes. It is estimated that at this point the McKenzie brothers had 400–500 head of cattle between them. A list prepared in 1923, when the brothers were seeking business partners, showed 125 Hereford-cross cows with 100 calves, 75 yearlings, 180 cattle of various ages, four Hereford-cross bulls and two purebred Hereford bulls.[19]

The brothers were short on capital and appear to have run their land at something of a subsistence level. In 1916 they

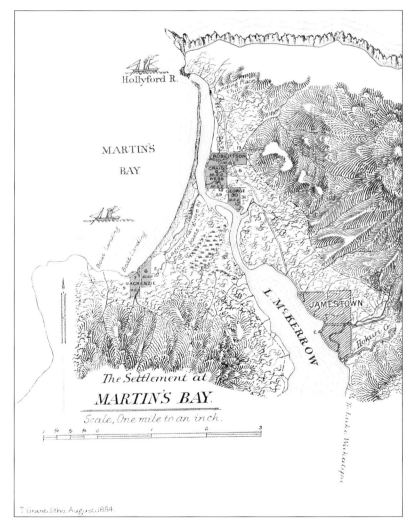

A map of the settlement at Martins Bay in 1884. The McKenzies' sections are marked on the south side of Martins Bay. Davey's base was on John George's section (No. 30, slightly above the centre of the map), although initially he used the old McKenzie homestead as well.

AJHR, 1884, Vol. 1, p. 73

Hugh (left) and Malcolm
McKenzie during the late
1930s.
Arnold Grey

were reported to be driving 30–40 cattle out to the market at
Mossburn, an undertaking that took about a month. The cattle
drives may have been done only once every two years, because
when climber Samuel Turner met the McKenzies in 1922 they
told him they had seen no one for two years except officers from
the *Hinemoa*, which called two or three times a year.[20]

The McKenzies' leases were mortgaged to the National
Mortgage and Agency Company of New Zealand. According
to Forest Service correspondence, the NMA was disappointed
in the lack of improvements in the runs and the small number
of cattle being brought to market.[21] The company was probably
pressing the men for better returns.

When the brothers visited Queenstown in May 1926, Hugh,
who had not been 'out' since March 1925, found that the
Department of Lands and Survey had issued a final notice in
April 1926 for arrears on rent payments for the Big Bay and
Kaipo runs.[22] Malcolm was also in arrears for rent payments
on his runs, although no final demand had yet been issued.
Things were looking rather desperate. Soon after their arrival
in Queenstown the *Lake Wakatip Mail* ran an article on the
brothers, who were quoted as saying they had 500–600 cattle and
had managed to get 150 'across the lower Pyke', which they
would take to the market in the spring.[23]

Notwithstanding the apparently exaggerated figures, the
NMA refused to lend them money to pay their rent arrears.

The McKenzies now had little choice but to sell the leases, and the NMA was keen to help, in order to recover its investment. In due course the properties came to attention of Patrick Fraser and Davey Gunn.[24]

Fraser may have been the man who showed Davey photos of the Hollyford and persuaded him that it would be 'a great spec'.[25] If so, then he chose his partner well. Davey was the perfect man for the job. Although he had limited experience with cattle, he was young and vigorous, prepared to work hard for little short-term gain, and enjoyed his own company.

Fraser, who was 44, had probably known Davey for years. Both had been born in the Waitaki Valley and the two families would certainly have been acquainted. In February 1902, just before he turned 20, Patrick enlisted with the North Otago Mounted Rifles and embarked a month later for South Africa and the Boer War. He returned just five months later, having arrived too late to see much action. His service records describe him as being five foot 11 inches tall, with a fair complexion, fair hair and grey eyes.[26]

Fraser followed his father in becoming a blacksmith, and by 1907, when he married Dempster Johnston, he was a blacksmith and engineer at Outram, about 50 kilometres from Sutton. When Davey moved to Sutton in 1919, he and Patrick became

A bull being delivered to Martins Bay for the McKenzie brothers from the government ship *Tutanekai* in 1925.

re-acquainted. At the time the two men went to the Hollyford, Fraser had four children, aged 13 to 17, who remained with their mother at Outram.[27]

It is likely that Patrick Fraser and Davey Gunn had a rose-tinted view of the Hollyford proposition. Did they know that the leases they had purchased were either close to expiring or only let on a year-to-year basis? Maybe they regarded this as no problem because pastoral leases were almost always renewed. What they may not have thought about was the growing interest in setting aside parts of New Zealand's back country for preservation and recreation. The concept of national parks became popular in the late 1800s, and Tongariro National Park, the fourth to be established in the world, was officially created in 1894. After the passage of the Scenery Preservation Act in 1903 an enormous area – 940,000 acres – was set aside in Fiordland with the intention of forming another national park, although this would not be officially constituted until 1952.[28]

Furthermore, in 1919 a large area north of Milford, including the Big Bay and Kaipo runs, had been set aside as provisional state forest. In the same year the Department of Lands and Survey moved to change the terms on these two runs from 14-year leases to year-to-year leases, so they could act quickly when the area was confirmed as a state forest.[29] It is possible that Fraser and Davey knew nothing about this proposal when they took over.

An idea of what the Hollyford would have been like when

Patrick Fraser at Pyke Hut in 1926. The new hut on the right was being built by Hugh and Malcolm McKenzie.

Murray Gunn Collection

the two first travelled there can be gleaned from George Moir's *Guide Book to the Tourist Routes of the Great Southern Lakes and Fiords of Western Otago* (1925), which described the dwellings in the Hollyford at the time. After descending into the Hollyford Valley from the Greenstone Saddle, the first was Middle or Mid Hut, which was situated near Moraine Creek and was described as being constructed of ponga trunks with a 'rubberoid roof' and room for five people on bunks and two more on the floor. The second hut, at Hidden Falls, was made of corrugated iron and could sleep the same number. Ten kilometres further on there was another hut, at Pyke River (above its confluence with the Hollyford), which had bunks for six but, Moir's guide stated, 'care must be taken when using the fireplace which is made of wood protected with stones around the hearth'. At the head of Lake McKerrow (10 kilometres from Pyke Hut) was an old surveyor's hut, which was 'comfortable but small'.[30]

Gordon Speden checking Davey's potato crop at Middle (Mid) Hut, December 1932.
Gordon Speden Collection

From McKerrow Hut a track followed the edge of Lake McKerrow to Martins Bay. There were two buildings here: the old McKenzie homestead and John George's house. George, who had farmed (mostly sheep) at Martins Bay for 25 years, had left in about 1902. Some 18 kilometres north-east around the coast from Martins Bay was Big Bay Hut, built by Ted Green in about 1903. At the time Davey took over the lease it may have been a one-room slab hut. Later photos show a corrugated-iron porch and a room built out of ponga logs.

With no road access into the Hollyford Valley, it made sense for the men to base themselves at Martins Bay, as the McKenzies had done. They used both the old homestead and George's house. Although the former was falling into disrepair, it had the important advantage of being near the dilapidated shed in the corner of the bay where the government steamer came in.

Davey and Fraser had arranged for the *Hinemoa* to drop stores when it passed by every four months. The first delivery was a disaster, as the men were absent and returned to find the stores ruined by the weather. The crew had put the supplies in the old shed but had not covered them with a tarpaulin and the shed roof had leaked. Delivery of stores was to be an ongoing problem; if the sea was rough and a dinghy unable to land in the bay, the steamer would simply carry on and try again four months later.[31]

An early photo of the hut at Big Bay. The back section was built by Ted Green in about 1902, and the ponga section was probably added by Davey. Note the potato patch.

Murray Gunn Collection

Once Davey and Fraser had finished exploring their land they started to tackle the enormous amount of work there was to do. The yards were run down and the flats were reverting to native bush. As we have seen, only about 1,000 of their 45,000 acres was in open country, and cattle numbers were low. Jim Lumsden (who was in the Hollyford in 1927–28) said it was impossible to get an accurate tally, but there were about 400 cattle ranging over the entire lease area. Many of these, he said, were 'clear-skins' (cattle that had never been marked), and 'they were a wild and difficult lot to handle'. The two men's first aim was to build up the herd, and that meant making more grazing land.[32]

They set about clearing scrub at Martins Bay, a task that was not without perils. Sometime during 1927 Davey badly cut his left hand with a slash-hook. He was on horseback cutting branches when his mount shied and he slashed through his ulnar artery. He bound the wound up with a towel, and when it was still troubling him a few days later, he unwrapped his hand and saw that it was green and smelly. Deciding that Davey needed medical attention, Fraser set off with him for Queenstown. The two men were held up by flooded rivers and it was five days before they finally arrived at Dr Anderson's, as the doctor recalled:[33]

> When they arrived in my surgery the blood-soaked towels were as hard as concrete, and it took a long time to soak

them off. When getting down toward the hand the stench was dreadful and the window of the surgery had to be opened.[34]

Dr Anderson was appalled at the state of Davey's hand and thought he might have to amputate it in order to save his life. This was in the days before antibiotics, and Davey was in danger of dying from blood poisoning. He was admitted to Frankton Hospital and had his hand immersed continuously in a hot iodine bath. After several weeks his hand recovered, with no loss of function but with a large scar.[35]

Davey and Ethel's younger daughter, Dorothy, recalled that one of her earliest memories of her father was when he came home to Oamaru after being discharged from hospital. 'He would put a bowl of water on the gas ring, turn it on and hold his hand in the water as long as he could. I imagine that it got quite hot before he gave in and removed it.'[36]

When Patrick Fraser left the Hollyford after just over a year, his share of the leases was transferred to Davey, on 3 November 1927.[37] Perhaps Fraser had decided the Hollyford was not, in fact, 'a great spec', but would entail years of hard graft for very little gain. Fraser initially returned to his family in Outram but later left them to live in Auckland.[38]

His departure meant a large extra call on Davey's finances and the loss of half of the workforce. Davey had been hoping to buy some more land at Martins Bay, in particular the 100

Davey's base at Martins Bay in about the 1930s.

Gordon Speden Collection

acres still owned by the McKenzie family, But this fell through, probably for lack of funds. Instead, he leased the land from the McKenzies for £5 a year.[39]

By now Davey had fallen in love with the Hollyford and it is doubtful that he ever considered leaving, even at this early stage. He had seen the potential and had great plans for improving the cattle-raising business. He was alive to the beauty of the district and wanted to make the area accessible to tourists, which he hoped would also improve his income.

Chapter Two

The Depression Years

His already difficult financial position will become quite hopeless.[1]

It was difficult for one man to work the runs on his own, and it was impossible to muster cattle in the Hollyford singlehanded. There was also plenty of track and building work to be done. After Fraser's departure Davey had a series of hired hands, including Jim Lumsden (Owaka), Alex McAlpine (Karamea) and Hughie Glass, a well-known North Canterbury blade-shearer. These men set about repairing holding paddocks and felling bush in the Pyke for fences. Later they cleared a 70-acre block at Big Bay.

The legendary prospector William O'Leary, or Arawata Bill as he was more commonly known, was based in the district, and later, during the 1930s, he worked for Davey, mostly looking after the huts and making sure they were stocked with firewood.[2]

Davey near Mid Hut, 1935.
Gordon Speden Collection

Davey's brother Robert (Bob) came to help out after Fraser left but did not stay long. Bob was 12 years younger and, as Davey had gone to live with his aunts around the time of Bob's birth, the pair were not close. The brothers had quite different temperaments; Bob, being the baby of the family, had been spoilt by his parents and sisters and could also be bad-tempered.[3] According to Bob's son Doug, early on in his time in the Hollyford his father ended up getting into a fight with one of Davey's men and promptly left.[4]

Together with his workers, Davey made some significant improvements. Instead of using the ailing Mid Hut, Davey built a timber-slab hut across the river from Deadmans Bluff, and this soon became known as Deadmans Hut.[5] The small and decrepit Pyke Hut was replaced with a new one, built by Hugh and Malcolm McKenzie, who worked for Davey on a casual basis for a number of years.[6] Clearings were made around existing huts and in other promising areas, and the ground was sprinkled with clover and cocksfoot seed.[7] Davey always had a pocket full of clover seeds and would sprinkle these wherever he thought they might grow.[8]

In 1927 the Forest Service was planning to lease out its land in the new state forest at Martins Bay. They were keen for the land to be occupied, even if the rent received was very low, because they were interested in the timber potential of the area, and needed tracks and huts to work from. As the Conservator explained: 'The lessee must for his own purposes keep open and maintain

The Pyke River could be crossed either via a wire rope and chair or by dinghy.
Lakes District Museum EL1562

A riding party at Deadmans Hut in February 1937.

Gordon Speden Collection

approximately 110 miles of tracks, some six or eight huts and two boats', and these would be of great benefit to the Forest Service.[9]

In December 1927 the Conservator of Forests for Southland informed his superior in Wellington that 'a good deal of personal feeling' had arisen between Davey and Malcolm McKenzie. The Conservator stated that McKenzie had misrepresented to Davey the extent and possibilities of the rights he was selling, and also that McKenzie was 'sore at losing the area'. McKenzie was apparently encouraging people to apply for grazing rights for small areas that were 'sandwiched between Gunn's rights'. The Conservator suggested that the whole area be offered to Davey without calling for tenders. Head office, however, was not prepared to deviate from standard procedure and replied that the grazing rights had to be advertised. In May 1928 advertisements duly appeared, calling for tenders for a year-to-year lease on state forest land at Martins Bay and around the coast to Big Bay, the boundary being the southern edge of Run 492. In the event, Davey's tender was the only one received and he was able to lease the 20,450 acres for £10 per year, giving him a total of over 65,000 acres of grazing land.[10]

If the issue of having most of his cattle run as year-to-year leases bothered Davey, he must have been relieved when his 14-year leases on the Hollyford runs (471–474) were changed to 21-year leases when they were renewed in March 1929.[11]

Davey (left) at Pyke Hut
(the third on this site) with
unknown mountaineer and
guide, about 1938.

Gordon Speden Collection

In January 1929 Davey met the first tourists to visit Martins
Bay since he and Fraser had arrived in 1926.[12] Eric James, pro-
prietor of a horse-trekking business in Okuru, arrived with a
small group he had brought down the coast from Haast. Davey
outlined to James his 'ambitious' plans for the area, and it is clear
from James's account of the visit that Davey was working hard
to get the place into shape. Wherever the riding party went they
saw evidence of new or re-cut tracks, found huts well stocked
with provisions and utensils, and saw recently cleared areas that
had been sown with clover and cocksfoot. New yards had been
erected at John George's old homestead at Martins Bay, although
James was surprised to see that the straining posts were made
of fuchsia timber, which he said was quite unsuitable, and unnecessary given the vast quantity of superior timber available.
When questioned about this, Davey explained that he had yet
to learn the different varieties and characteristics of West Coast
timber.[13]

When the Wall Street stockmarket crashed in October
1929 Davey was probably at Martins Bay, and would not have
learned about the calamitous events until he went out just before
Christmas to visit his family. When he stopped at Elfin Bay Station
before catching a steamer to Queenstown, he would have been
told the bad news by George and Annie Shaw.

Davey's family were under the impression that the subsequent
Depression did not affect him. His son Murray later recalled: 'He

didn't feel the Depression. He was living a pretty primitive life anyway; all he needed was stores and the rest was work, work, work.'[14] In fact, it took Davey years to recover from the financial impact. The timing could not have been worse. He had spent a couple of hard years building up cattle numbers and investing capital into his venture. By 1929 he was probably in a position to start bringing out reasonable numbers of sale cattle, but now stock prices were plummeting and Davey's annual turnover dropped from an already modest £900 a year to about £200.[15]

Luckily, he had few outgoings. He wasn't buying fertiliser, stock or fencing materials, and even for his new huts he mostly made do with recycled materials. But even with these economies the drop in stock prices hit him hard. After he had decreased his debt with the NMA during 1928 and 1929 (to £957), it climbed steadily during the early 1930s and to almost £2,000 by 1934. Things were so bad that at times he was reduced to eating porridge for both breakfast and dinner. (Davey didn't hold with stopping for a meal in the middle of the day.)[16]

In August 1931 trampers Lindsay McCurdy and Jack Dobbie met Davey Gunn, Malcolm McKenzie and Arawata Bill

Davey (left) with his good friend George Shaw (of Elfin Bay Station) at the head of the East Eglinton during the early 1930s.

Gordon Speden Collection

Davey with his workers at Martins Bay in September 1931. From left: S. Shaw, Leo Keheller, Davey, Malcolm McKenzie and C. Keheller.

Mary Thomson

at Martins Bay. The locals had seen no one for five months and McCurdy recorded that the conversation was all about the Depression, 'bad government and the Dole'.[17]

In 1931 Davey was unable to pay the rates due to the Lake County Council.[18] By March 1932 he was having difficulty paying his lease fees and was having penalties added to his outstanding account. The arrears were held over pending the sale of cattle, but in February 1933 the Commissioner of Crown Lands wrote to advise Davey that the leases would be cancelled if the outstanding amount was not paid:[19]

> . . . your rights to occupy under the two Miscellaneous Licences are from year-to-year only, and if rent is not paid on due date then the licences automatically lapse . . . I should be glad if you would endeavour to liquidate these arrears as early as possible; otherwise it may be necessary to submit your case to the Land Board for action detrimental to your interests.[20]

Despite the tough talk, the Commissioner refrained from taking any action 'in view of the present difficult times', but by the end of May 1933 Davey's licence had lapsed.[21] In November 1933 he sold 64 cattle for £300. Hearing of this, the Commissioner again pressed the NMA (Davey's agent and financier) for payment.[22] The NMA refused, presumably not wishing to increase Davey's debt to them at a time when so many farmers owed so much.

Davey's debt to the NMA was reducing by only a small amount each year. In 1933, for example, his farming venture made a profit of £165 (the average wage was about £350[23]), but the NMA was paying Ethel £156 a year on Davey's behalf, so his debt would have been reduced by only £9.[24]

In a desperate bid in November 1934, Davey drove his cattle all the way to the Burnside saleyards near Dunedin rather than taking them to Lorneville, presumably in the hope of a better price.[25] This must have been a huge logistical exercise, and Davey was reliant on the goodwill of many farmers along the way to feed and water his stock. He sold 60 cattle for £272 and visited the Commissioner of Crown Lands to inform him of the fact. Some money was forthcoming from the NMA a few weeks later, but it was to take Davey another few years to clear his arrears completely.[26]

The Depression had at least one positive spin-off. The relief work schemes included road-building, and in 1929–30 a road was built from Te Anau to the Te Anau Downs Station (30 kilometres). By 1934 the road had reached as far as The Divide (85

Ruth Benstead at Davey's hut in the Upper Pyke, about 1943.

Gordon Speden Collection

kilometres), and it then began to descend into the Hollyford Valley. Marian Camp was built where the road reached the Hollyford River and began to follow the river up to the Homer Tunnel.[27] From 1936 a road began to creep down the Hollyford Valley towards Deadmans Hut, and this would eventually provide an easier route for droving cattle to the saleyards.

The McKenzies and Ted Green had taken their cattle out via the Hollyford Valley, over the Greenstone Saddle and then down the Greenstone Valley.[28] This was not an easy undertaking, and the most difficult part was along the side of Lake McKerrow, a route later named the 'Demon Trail' by Jim Speden. Lake McKerrow is 15 kilometres long, and the track climbs up and over every one of the numerous spurs that come down into the lake. Horses would try to double back, so it must have been hard work keeping a mob of unenthusiastic cattle moving. If you lost cattle here, and they headed for the tops, you might never see them again. Davey decided soon after arriving in the Hollyford that it would be easier to get his cattle out via the Pyke River. The added bonus was that he could open up new grazing land as well.

Further impetus was given to the work when Malcolm McKenzie attempted to secure a lease in the Pyke Valley during the early 1930s. McKenzie's application was declined and Davey's friends in the Forest Service issued a lease to him instead. In late 1933 Malcolm McKenzie and two others applied for a lease over an area near the Hackett River, north of Big Bay, where they wanted to muster wild cattle and then fatten them up before driving them out to Mossburn. Southland's Conservator of Forests wrote to his counterpart in Hokitika, whose jurisdiction covered the area applied for by McKenzie, arguing against this application:

> From the Service and Lands Department point of view, the lease of areas in this locality to persons other than Mr Gunn appears undesirable as, should he be compelled to fence or otherwise define his boundaries or keep his stock within strict limits, his already difficult financial position will become quite hopeless, and he must abandon the whole area. It is extremely doubtful if a more suitable lessee could be found.[29]

Davey built this hut on the Barrier River flats in 1935. This photo was taken in about 1952.

Ed Cotter

Meanwhile, Davey was already making the area his own, by building tracks around Lake Alabaster and Lake Wilmot and picking routes around several large swamps in the Pyke Valley. Some parts of the track around Lake Wilmot were hewn from solid rock, involving the use of explosives. Between 1927 and 1931 Davey received government grants totalling £250 for making and repairing tracks, and most of this work was carried on in the Pyke Valley. In January 1934 mountaineer Alex Dickie noted that the track up the Pyke River from the head of Lake Alabaster had been made 'within the last year or two' and 'was a real pleasure to travel on'. A few months later, Lindsay McCurdy described the track around Lake Alabaster as 'pretty rough' and said that 'the track around Lake Wilmot is new but is very rough', so perhaps Davey had already taken a mob of cattle out this way.[30]

A new stock route required new huts, and in the Upper Pyke, near where the track branches off to Big Bay, McCurdy 'came to stockyards and a new hut of Mr Gunn's'. Another tramper remarked that at this hut 'slabs of tree trunks did service for walls and table'. In 1935 a totara-slab hut was built near the Barrier River:[31]

[Upper Pyke Hut] is a modern slab-built place without a

window. Enough daylight filters through between the slabs, and the smoke keeps out the sandflies. The hut is remote enough to justify the absence of a window.[32]

Building a hut in such a remote locality was no easy task, and Davey made use of whatever he had to hand. Trees were felled, trimmed and then snigged out of the bush by horse. Nails, roofing iron and windows would all have to be packed to the site, either from the boat landing at Martins Bay or via the Greenstone Valley. Davey recycled wherever possible, straightening out nails and flattening corrugated iron so that he would get more cover. Fortunately, he was a good axeman and enjoyed working with timber. The beech uprights and beams in the Upper Pyke and Barrier Huts were said to be so square they could almost have passed for mill-sawn timber.[33]

Davey was generous about the use of his facilities. In about 1931 brothers David and Roy McDonald, along with several others (including Gunn employee Tip Cashmore and Malcolm and Hugh McKenzie), were prospecting for gold on the remote Madagascar Beach, between Martins Bay and Milford Sound.[34] In 1932 George Lindsay and Malcolm McKenzie continued their work, and were later joined by Kenneth McAlpine, T. Courtenay and E. Martin.[35] These parties were eventually defeated by the isolation and difficult terrain, but when they were travelling through the Hollyford they enjoyed free use of Davey's huts and the dinghy on Lake McKerrow. Davey must also have supplied the parties with some food. They invariably turned up at Martins Bay starving, having travelled for several days with very few supplies. David McDonald, who walked out via the Hollyford, recorded being pleased to find potatoes at Deadmans Hut, which were a welcome addition to his pigeon soup.[36]

Later in the 1930s Malcolm McKenzie became excited about the possibility of oil at Madagascar Beach and, together with Queenstown men Gerald Sharpe and Benny Angelo, spent a lot of time in the area. The three became known as the 'Oil Kings', and again Davey supported them in their endeavours, although yet again they came to nothing.[37]

It was in 1934 that Davey finally became aware, if he did not already know, that having year-to-year leases was problematic. When he arrived in Oamaru in November he received notification that the grazing licence on Run 492 (Big Bay, 16,900

acres) was to be cancelled.[38] In his slow but neat hand Davey wrote a strongly worded letter to the Commissioner of Crown Lands in Dunedin, protesting against the 'Tourist Department' taking possession of land that he had 'been breaking in for the past 8 years' and that he had 'just got . . . workable'. He had built a hut in the Pyke and had a fair-size clearing that he had sown in grass. In any case, he said, he had 'never known tourists to go on that side of the river'.[39] In January 1935 he was advised that the licence on Run 495 (Kaipo Valley, 1,500 acres) would also not be renewed when it expired in six months. 'The area in question,' wrote the Conservator of Forests, 'has been withdrawn from State Forest reservation and set aside for the purpose of a National Park.'[40]

In June 1935 Davey was able to take up his lapsed year-to-year lease on the 20,450 acres in the Martins Bay district, for which he had been unable to pay the rent during the Depression. The Forest Service then decided to expand the licence to include Run 492 (at Big Bay), the land on both sides of the Pyke River above Lake Alabaster, and also some land up the lower Olivine and Barrier Rivers. All up this was 71,000 acres and was

The 'Oil Kings' on the beach at Big Bay. From left: Gerald Sharpe, Benny Angelo and Malcolm McKenzie.

Arthur Bradshaw Collection

good value at £20 a year, although it was still only a yearly lease. There is no evidence that Davey was able to get another lease for the 1,500 acres in the lower Kaipo Valley (Run 495), but he continued to graze this area (and the upper valley, for which he had never had a licence) until his death.[41]

Davey received and posted letters concerning his leases when he visited Oamaru every six months or so. According to son Murray, in the way of things at the time, his father was very secretive about financial matters and told his wife nothing.

In early 1936 Davey began writing to the Marine Department about the dilapidated state of the landing shed at Martins Bay. This letter of July 1937 was his fifth on the subject, and although the Marine Department priced materials and budgeted for the expense, World War Two intervened and the work was never done.

Archives New Zealand/Te Rua Mahara o te Kawanatanga, Wellington Office, M 1, 3/13/674 (ADOE 16612)

In November or December, after Davey had brought cattle out to the saleyards, he would travel to Oamaru and stay with his family for a week or two. He would turn up again for another short break during the winter months, having left his horses and dogs at Elfin Bay Station with the Shaw family.

Daughter Dorothy remembered that the children revered their father: 'Looking back, what we felt for our father was hero worship – after all, we only saw him twice a year for about two weeks each time.'[43]

In 1937 Murray contracted scarlet fever and was seriously ill. His mother Ethel sent a telegram to the Shaws. George Shaw immediately went out to reshoe his horse while Annie packed up a week's worth of food for him. George left at noon, rode 25 kilometres that afternoon and started again at dawn the next day. He spent another two days riding before finding Davey. A couple of days later the pair arrived back at Elfin Bay in the middle of the night, and the following day Davey caught the steamer to Queenstown and carried on to Oamaru.[44]

Murray remembered that his father turned up in about 1937 or 1938 with the perfect imprint of a horseshoe on the top of his head, adding to his hero status in the eyes of his children:

> He didn't tell stories about the Hollyford when he came home. He brought a greenstone adze home and he gave it to me and then the next day he gave it away to my uncle, which upset me a lot. He bought exotic things home like kea feathers, a tusk off a little seal, bits of greenstone, bits of gold in bottles.[42]

By the mid-1930s Davey had a thousand head of cattle. He had survived the Depression and, thanks to the public works schemes, enjoyed easier access to his stock. His lifestyle had made him exceptionally fit, he loved 'his' Hollyford and the runs were probably profitable. In addition he was starting to make a small income from letting tourists use his new huts, and by working as a guide when requested.

Davey and Ethel's marriage had reached an impasse. She refused to go to the Hollyford, claiming it was too rough, and it became increasingly clear that he had no plans to leave. Davey had made his choice: he was wedded to the Hollyford.

Chapter Three

Davey the Man

He was made of horseshoe nails and whipcord.[1]

In 1936 Davey had been farming in the Hollyford for 10 years. He was 49 years old. The Hollyford had perhaps not turned out quite as well financially as he had anticipated, but the future looked promising.

Davey was entirely comfortable with his simple, intensely physical life. He was not a tall man – about five foot seven (170 centimetres) – and was always described as wiry. At 49 he was still lean and very fit and strong. He moved slowly but easily and didn't expend energy unnecessarily. His hands were well worn from the hard physical work he loved. Good hard work was, he said, a way to right living. His grey-blue eyes often had a twinkle.[2] His friend Gordon Speden recalled that 'Dave was a mass of energy, physically and mentally, always on the move from daylight to well after darkness had fallen. As soon as he opened an eye to find it daylight he was on the move.'[3]

Davey's son Murray also remembered his father's physical prowess:

> When I was about nine we were going down the street, we were only a block and a half from the shops, and he said 'I'll race you' and he tore off down the road with me trailing behind. He would have been about 48, as fit as a buck rat.[4]

Although a modest man, Davey was quietly proud of his fitness and would compete with younger men. Doug Gunn, son of Davey's younger brother Bob, went to work for his uncle just after the war when Davey was about 58 and Doug was 24.

Davey at 50 years of age. This photo was taken on the occasion of Arthur Bradshaw landing the first plane at Martins Bay in May 1937.

Arthur Bradshaw Collection

Davey at Martins Bay, his favourite place. This photo was taken by Elsie K. Morton, who hand-coloured it and gave it to him as a gift.
Murray Gunn Collection

As they travelled down the valley they came across two trees that had fallen over the track. Davey took the slightly bigger one, and the two started and finished chopping at the same time.[5]

Davey never grew a beard because he found it uncomfortable. When he was younger he shaved once a week while mustering and every three or four days when he was at base camp. Although his hair remained dark as he aged, his whiskers began to grow white and in the latter years of his life he began to shave every day. He had always looked younger than he was and he wanted to keep it that way.[6]

He was constantly extolling the grandness of the Hollyford but also revelled in tiny examples of the simple beauty around him, such as the perfection of a tiny crab skeleton found on the beach.[7] Being in the Hollyford allowed Davey to meet others with a similar love of the outdoors, and he formed many life-long friendships. Although happy with his own company, he wasn't a loner. He enjoyed company and had no difficulty relating to women. He was always welcoming to visitors and was very hospitable, invariably offering shelter and sustenance.

An unnamed tramper, writing in the jubilee edition of the *Southland Tramper*, recalled the first time he met Davey, near McKerrow Hut. He remembered Davey's 'friendly smile and quiet greeting that made us feel not just another pair of

Normally quiet and self-contained, Davey was always happy to socialise with friends.

Derek and Pat Turnbull Collection

schoolboys a long way from home, but one of a brotherhood and welcome in the Hollyford'.[8]

Despite his friendly manner, Davey was quietly spoken and laconic. With close friends he might have been slightly more forthcoming, but he still never discussed his feelings or any problems.[9] As well as being the norm for a 'Kiwi bloke' at the time, this was probably also a result of his upbringing. Davey's mother was a kind and loving woman, but his father had always been frugal with praise and had high expectations of his first-born son. When he was 12 Davey was sent to live with his two maiden aunts at Hook Bush, near Waimate, to be 'the man about the place'. The aunts were good to him, but he was the only child and spent a lot of time by himself roaming the hills, and obviously learned to keep his thoughts to himself.[10] There were, though, exceptions to Davey's reserve. Murray remembered that there was nothing his father liked more than a lively, intelligent discussion:

> He seemed very off-hand with people around him, like employees, but when somebody came along from the professions [doctors, botanists, geologists, etc.] he livened up straight away and was all over them and they were all over him. He had different things to discuss with them that he couldn't discuss with the people around him. He kept very aloof if you were working here. Well-educated people he enjoyed better than anything.[11]

Davey didn't waste words and even the most unusual happenings would warrant only a few of them. When writer Rupert Sharpe was working in the Hollyford the mustering party startled a stag in the bush and somehow the animal got its antlers tangled in supplejack. In the ensuing chaos of excited dogs and men it was impossible to shoot the stag, but it was still kicking wildly and the men could not get near. After a struggle it was eventually killed with a butcher's knife. Musterer Jim Sinclair suggested to Sharpe that the incident might make a good story for the paper he wrote for. 'Humph!' snorted Davey, overhearing. 'I couldn't write ten words about it.'[12]

Compliments and praise did not come easily to Davey. Sharpe spent several months mustering with him in 1949 and described how Davey once stopped a yearling bull making a dash for freedom: 'For the first and last time I had heard Dave make a complimentary remark. "That was a good stop," he said. Then, as though abashed at his own generosity, he added: "That's the way a man can get hurt, sometimes." '[13]

But if he wasn't generous with praise, Davey didn't bawl his staff out either. Alan Snook, one of Davey's teenage hands, could not remember ever being told off by his employer. Davey also never gave orders to his workers. He would mention that a job needed to be done and wait for the men to offer to do it.[14]

To his younger employees he was Mr Gunn, and he had no time to chat. Alan Snook was 15 when he went to work for Davey in about 1938, and said that Davey 'only told me things that he thought I should know'. Davey was, however, willing to make allowances for youth. He himself never stopped for lunch, and Snook went along with this for a few days, but it was hard going for a 15-year-old doing strenuous work. Finally he said, 'Mr Gunn, I just can't go on like this, you're killing me.' The next day Davey, who must have baked a loaf of bread late at night, gave Snook a packet of golden-syrup sandwiches wrapped in newspaper.[15]

Davey charming Miss Grant of Gore at the old McKenzie homestead, Martins Bay, about 1941.

Murray Gunn Collection

There are many stories of Davey's stubbornness, including this one from son Murray:

> Jack [Jenkins] and my father were down at Hidden Falls and after some heavy rain a gut had appeared across the track and it needed a footbridge. Jack wanted to put it on the main track but my father wanted to put it in the bush about 20 feet away. They didn't argue – they just went and built two bridges. I came out on a muster with Ed Cotter and my father. Ed was leading a horse and the cattle had got used to following the horse. My father was behind, forcing the cattle on by getting the dogs to bark at them. Ed took Jack's bridge on the main track, the cattle followed Ed's horse, the dogs followed the cattle and my father took his own little bridge. If he hadn't had that stubbornness he couldn't have existed [in the Hollyford].[16]

Davey's workers soon learned not to waste their breath offering advice or suggestions. Murray recalled: 'If you were working with him and there was an obvious way to do a job, he'd always find an alternative. He wouldn't tolerate you doing it your own way.'[17]

Rupert Sharpe told an illuminating story about the erection of a hitching rail near Big Bay Hut. Davey had mentioned several times that the job needed doing, and finally the day came when Sharpe had time to do it. Davey suggested he get some broadleaf posts from the bush. Sharpe found some suitable trees, chopped them down and carried the heavy, wet posts back to the hut one at a time. He dug holes and rammed the posts in tight, while Davey pottered around the hut and observed progress without comment. Soon after, Jim Sinclair arrived and he and Sharpe were chatting about the job when Jim asked where Davey was. Sharpe had not noticed the latter's absence.

> . . . about thirty minutes later he staggered out . . . On his shoulder there was a broadleaf post about twice as big as any of the three I had just rammed in their holes. To find out what was in his mind I had to ask a lot of questions, but eventually I dug out the three posts I had planted and replaced them with three more, each one cut and carried by that peculiar old battler, Dave Gunn.[18]

Davey was quite comfortable carrying heavy logs.
Murray Gunn Collection

From all reports, Davey was even-tempered and unflapp-able. Musterer Ian Haggitt recalled him fending off a charging cattlebeast by kicking at it while sitting on a log. Even the most startling news would only provoke a long 'Ohhhh'. When Alan de la Mare went down the Hollyford in 1941, his party carried with them a 12-volt battery for the launch. When the group reached Martins Bay they found the launch full of water that had to be bailed out. Salty water also had to be drained from the engine. The job done, one of the group put the head back on the engine, but he didn't tighten the bolts properly and the head cracked. De la Mare was amazed when Davey didn't get angry. He simply said, 'Oh well, I'm going to have to get another head for it,' which de la Mare knew would take at least another three months.[19]

Davey was a Labour Party supporter, which some of his farming friends found hard to understand. In matters of faith he described himself as agnostic, and if people questioned him he would say, 'Yes, there is a God, but you prove it to me.' The Reverend Kerr, a Presbyterian minister from Wallacetown, used to come to the Hollyford and would say a prayer for Davey, which Davey endured but did not like. He was proud of his Scottish ancestry. His father 'had the Gaelic', and Davey would often use the phrase 'Slàinte mhath' (Good health). He was fond of bagpipe music and was described as almost worshipping Robbie Burns. He also enjoyed the Australian bush poet Banjo Paterson, and especially liked the poem 'Clancy of the Overflow', which he could relate to, having worked in an office and chosen to be a cowboy instead.[20]

But it was Davey's toughness and strength that impressed the young men who worked for him. Musterer Brian Swete remembered him as 'the toughest man I have known. Jack Jenkins, who was perhaps the second-toughest man I have known, described Dave as being made of horseshoe nails and whipcord.'[21]

In about 1947 Davey and his nephew Doug set off one morning from Deadmans with a mob of cattle bound for the Lorneville saleyards. Something spooked the cattle and three of them bolted into the bush. Davey set off after them on foot, but fell awkwardly on a sharp stick, which ripped through his trousers and tore his scrotum. Doug takes up the story:

> He came out of the bush and told me what had happened. I held the cattle while he got on his horse and rode back to Deadmans. He used some iodine and then stitched himself up. He then came back to me on his horse and chased the

The hitching rail at Big Bay in 1954. Note also the large addition to the hut (left) to provide sleeping quarters for guided walkers.

Ed Cotter

three cattle that had bolted. We had to start out again the next day and he never complained once on the rest of the drive, although he must have been in great pain.[22]

Davey recounted the story to Rupert Sharpe and Jim Sinclair (probably to shame Sinclair, whose leg had been punctured by a cow's horn, into not taking any time off). The wound, Davey concluded, 'healed up pretty good in the long run, but it was sore for a long time when I was riding a horse'. Sinclair never mentioned his own injury again.[23]

Accidents were common in the rough country, and Davey had his fair share. Ray Wilson, who was employed by the Public Works Department to supervise track improvements in the area, travelled with Davey from Big Bay to Martins Bay in about 1948. A young horse had followed them, determined to keep company with the horses the men were riding. Along the track near Long Reef Point they came to a narrow gut between two rocks. Davey would block this off when he wanted to stop cattle from going between Big Bay and Martins Bay. Wanting the young horse to stay on the Big Bay side, he set about placing timber posts in the gap. The horse, realising it was about to be thwarted, ran up and tried to jump over. It hit Davey in the chest and he was badly hurt. Wilson managed to get him to Martins Bay Hut, but it was obvious he needed medical attention.

The following day Wilson rowed Davey up the lake to McKerrow Hut, where there were more supplies. From there he rode out to Deadmans, and sent one of Davey's musterers back to the hut to look after Davey until he was able to travel out to the Hollyford Road and receive medical attention. It must have been a painful journey. Along with the more severe injuries mentioned in this book, Davey also broke his thumb, a finger, a small bone in his forearm and a bone in his foot, injuries for which he never sought any medical attention.[24]

Ian Haggitt recalled that Davey used a folded sugar bag to pad his shoulder when he carried a log. 'One day he brought a log in and dropped it for Gordon [Donaldson-Law] and me to carry it to the hut. It was all the two of us could do to lift it and totter along with it.'[25]

Davey would gladly share anything he had, but he was also extremely careful to avoid waste. Ray Wilson remembered Davey as:

the most generous of souls when he was out in civilisation. He would call at the Te Anau Hotel, put money on the bar and treat anyone, whether he knew them or not. However, the moment he got back into the Hollyford it would be a rare sight indeed to see him throw a penny's worth of anything out.[26]

Yet he had a relaxed attitude to cash, keeping his takings from the tourist operation in a large biscuit tin in a cupboard at Deadmans Hut, which any number of people could have helped themselves to. At the end of the season he was pleased if he had enough money in the tin to pay his bills.[27]

The Depression would have honed Davey's frugality, along with the difficulty of getting supplies in during the 1920s and 1930s, when the steamer visits were irregular. Having to eke out stores taught him to make do, and the habit became ingrained.[28]

On one occasion Davey and nephew Doug were away mustering and had taken with them a tin of butter. When they got to the hut at Barrier Flats, Davey found an old tin of butter he had left there many months before. He put the new tin in the cupboard and took out the old one to use. Doug refused to eat it, but Davey had no such qualms. He got stuck into the rancid butter while Doug ate from the new tin.[29]

Family friend Derek Turnbull remembered a time at Martins Bay Hut when the place was plagued with mice:

> Davey laid some strychnine around the hearth. He was cooking some meat and it fell on the hearth. Rather than waste it, Davey scraped it off and ate it. Afterwards he fell violently ill, so he put his fingers down his throat, threw up and survived. He wouldn't waste anything.[30]

Catching fish was fun until the men realised that they would be expected to eat fish for breakfast, lunch and dinner. Sometimes they would surreptitiously bury old meat or fish. Rupert Sharpe remembered the guilt they felt when Davey caught them in the act of cutting out maggoty meat from some venison haunches that had got a bit high:

> Gunn was clearly put out. Not, I felt, at the sight of the maggots, but more at the idea that anyone should distrust his care of the food he cooked for us. He was a good cook, and we

Davey would always mend and make do. Here he is repairing a saddle.
Murray Gunn Collection

didn't altogether distrust him at that, but in interfering with his meat we had overstepped our limits, and in spite of the crawling evidence Jim [Sinclair] and I felt guilty.[31]

Arthur Bradshaw had two vivid memories of Davey:

Firstly, if a cattlebeast died – he would never kill one – he would cut the meat into thin strips, dry them in the sun, and store them in his nearest hut. Then later, when he required a meal, he would soak some of the strips and cook them. Secondly was the cooking utensil he considered to be the most important item in each hut: the sifter, essential for sifting the mouse droppings out of the flour![32]

Davey's carefulness with resources extended to his cattle. He would spend hours rescuing a steer stuck in a mud-hole when most men would have shot it and used it for dog tucker.[33]

Tools that were important to him, such as axes and slashers, were well maintained, but Davey was not much interested in repairing buildings, boats and most other equipment.[34] If a repair was critical he would use whatever he had to hand – a piece of string, some flax or a length of wire.[35] The boats suffered most from Davey's benign neglect. A launch delivered by the government steamer in about 1938 and used on Lake McKerrow was described 10 years on as 'an amazingly dilapidated old boat'.[36]

Gordon Donaldson-Law tried to help:

> One of the things that struck me when I came into the Hollyford was the really bad condition of the horse tack. I suggested to Dave that I should oil and overhaul it, but Dave said, 'Ain't no good in this climate, it is cheaper to let it go and replace it.' The only trouble was that while he carried out the first part, he never fulfilled the second![37]

Time didn't mean much to Davey, who thought that if you arrived home in the dark, the day had been well spent. He once spent a whole rainy day chasing a couple of heifers up and down the side of Lake McKerrow and in and out of the water.

Davey enjoyed sharing the Hollyford with his friends. This photograph shows him with a group of Invercargill friends who were on their way to Martins Bay in late December 1937. From left: Jack Todd, Wattie Bews, Davey, Doug Robson.

Murray Gunn Collection

At the end of the day he said, 'Aw, I don't want them anyway but it will have educated them.' His men were unimpressed.[38]

After deciding to go somewhere, Davey would then muck around all morning, eventually setting off mid-afternoon. He liked to travel in the cool of the evening, and thought nothing of rowing down Lake McKerrow at night. He would usually arrive at huts after dark. Gordon Speden remembered Davey arriving at Barrier Hut at 2.30 a.m., having left Deadmans late in the afternoon.[39] This could be tough on those accompanying him, such as Ray Wilson:

> Dave always worked on the principle that . . . you never arrive at a hut with any daylight remaining. He was always reluctant to get an early start because he knew we'd arrive at the next hut before dark, so he would always find a loose shoe on the horse or something like that and he'd work on that or perhaps repairing a bit of harness. If we still made good time and there seemed to be the possibility of arriving in daylight he would ask you to wait for a quarter of an hour while he went to check some cattle . . . He'd be back in about an hour's time and then we'd ride on to the hut and duly arrive in the dark as usual.[40]

Workers on the property learned to set off on their own rather than waiting for Davey and having to ride for several hours in the dark. When Davey began running guided trips his guests would sometimes get annoyed by his late starts, especially if their time was limited.[41]

Davey was usually late in getting his cattle to the sale-yards at Lorneville. On one occasion, after he had persuaded his daughter Dorothy to time her wedding to coincide with the end of his cattle drive, he found that, as usual, he was running late. He had to engage a drover to take over the cattle while he rushed to the wedding in Oamaru.[42]

He enjoyed teasing his friends and visitors. Elisabeth Stuart-Jones, who walked the Hollyford in 1951, recalled that Davey woke them in the morning by pulling on their toes. He also thought it was great fun to push people's heads into the water when they were lying down having a drink from a stream.[43] A party trick for children was twisting his nose with one hand while making a cracking noise that sounded like his nose breaking.[44]

Davey dressed up for his daughter Dorothy's wedding at Oamaru, 1947.

Murray Gunn Collection

Davey with Ian Speden in the Hollyford Valley in 1943.

Gordon Speden Collection

Davey wouldn't laugh at people's mistakes, though he did like to pull people's legs. When you were going back to a hut in the dark he would deliberately try and get away from you. One time Davey was with someone who promoted themselves as a great walker. They were walking up the side of Lake McKerrow and Davey was in front. Every time Davey was out of sight of the walker he would run so that no matter how fast the walker went he kept getting further and further behind.[45]

Jean Prust, who knew Davey in the early 1950s, described him as having a quiet wit. On one occasion the members of a tramping club were discussing ballet. Someone jokingly asked Davey, 'Do you understand the choreography of the ballet?' 'No,' he replied, 'but I understand the geography of the valley.'[46]

Murray recalled that his father never told dirty jokes and very rarely swore. 'The only time I heard him swear was when he got to Pyke Hut and it had been left a mess by people. He picked up a spirtle and waved it around and said, "The buggers and the bastards. The buggers and the bastards."'[47]

Derek Turnbull, a family friend, recalled that Davey was very good with children.[48] For farm kids who were used to walking, riding and staying in huts, the Hollyford was one big adventure, and Davey was happy to spend time with them, taking them fishing and showing them around.

Arnold Grey lived in 1937–39 with his parents at Hendersons Camp, which was built in 1938 by the Public Works Department as accommodation for married men working on the Hollyford Road.[49] Grey remembered that he and his friend Bobby McKnight befriended Davey Gunn, who gave them a retired packhorse to ride. When Davey was due out, the boys would go down to Deadmans to collect wood and get the hut ready. Sometimes they would go down three or four days in a row before Davey would eventually arrive, 'but it was always a big adventure when he did'.[50]

Davey's relationship with his own children was more problematic. He didn't know them very well, and although they were sporty they weren't tough farm kids. Murray was just six months old when his father more or less disappeared from his life. Only Davey's eldest daughter, Isabel, could remember her father living at home. Murray once heard his father say that he was lonely being away from his children in the first year, but then he got used to it.[51]

When Davey did come to Oamaru, the children rushed to greet him. Relations between the Davey and Ethel appear to have remained friendly. Isabel thought that her mother 'didn't like [Davey being away] but was resigned to it'. The family always referred to Davey as either 'coming out' or 'going in', and it was only later that they found that some of their friends wondered if he was going in and out of jail![52]

When he was at Oamaru Davey did get involved in family

Davey visiting his family at Waimate but keeping his distance, about 1927. Ethel is holding Isabel, and Davey's sister Jean is standing behind their mother, Isabella.

Murray Gunn Collection

life. Dorothy remembered her father rubbing ointment onto her eczema with his work-roughened hands, which she said was 'like scratching but without the consequences'. Isabel remembered her father enjoying rubbing his whiskers across the children's faces.[53] Sometimes when Davey put the children to bed he would sing to them (very flat):

> On the ball
> On the ball
> On the ball
> Through centre three-quarters and all
> While sticking together
> We keep on the leather
> On the ball
> On the ball
> On the ball.

In Oamaru Davey also spent time visiting relations and friends. His sister Mary and her husband, George Meek, lived

Davey with son Murray (left) and daughter Dorothy during Dorothy's first visit to the Hollyford in 1941. The name of the man on the right is not known.

Murray Gunn Collection

in Wharf Street. George had worked at Galloway Station before he married, and he also worked at Dalgety's stock and station agency. He wrote essays and poetry, and Davey enjoyed his company immensely. He would also visit Donald Stronach, who had briefly owned the farm at Sutton after Davey. Stronach lived on a boat and had the reputation of being something of a play-boy, although he was a father figure to Murray.[54]

Davey also spent time catching up on the news, Dorothy recalled. 'I remember him sitting on the floor by the old news-paper cupboard and reading *all* the old newspapers from cover to cover, some probably at least a couple of months old.'[55] After a while he would catch the train from Oamaru to Waimate, where he would visit his mother and other sisters, and then more friends and relations.[56]

But Davey maintained that he never felt really well when he was in town, and before long he would head off again.[57] 'He quite enjoyed being out for a fortnight, he liked seeing his friends and reading the paper but a fortnight was enough.'[58] He would travel by train back to Queenstown, where he probably

Davey doesn't appear in any of the surviving family photos taken at Galloway Station, where his father was manager. This one, taken in about 1910, shows (from left): George Meek, Mary Meek and Jean Gunn (Davey's sisters), Bob Gunn (brother), Isabella and Alexander Gunn (parents).

Murray Gunn Collection

bought a few stores before getting on a steamboat to Elfin Bay Station. He would usually spend a night there with the Shaw family, before changing into his 'bush' clothes, saddling his horse and heading back into the Hollyford.

It was an unusual relationship, but his children didn't know any different:

> In the early days when my father came, he just turned up twice a year and we thought that was normal. He wasn't a father to us, he was a glamorous figure who came home and spent a short time with us . . . then he would just disappear back to the Hollyford, his beloved Hollyford.[59]

Chapter Four

The Legend Begins

An amazing feat: Three-day journey in 20 hours.[1]

The crash-landing of a Fox Moth aeroplane into the surf at Big Bay and Davey's actions after the event were the beginning of the Davey Gunn legend.

The 30th of December 1936 started ordinarily enough for Davey. He was at Martins Bay with a group of a dozen trampers whom he had guided down the valley and was now taking around to Big Bay. Most of the party were on foot, with packhorses carrying stores and personal gear. One of the group, a nurse called May Robbie, was due to fly out from Big Bay that afternoon and was to be replaced by another nurse, Catherine Buckingham, who was flying in on the same plane. The rendezvous was set for 4 p.m.[2]

The pilot of the Fox Moth was Arthur Bradshaw, who had founded Southland Airways in late 1935. Scenic flights were very popular during the mid-1930s and Bradshaw had flown frequently in the Mount Cook area, to Stewart Island and over Fiordland and Southland. Big Bay beach at low tide was one of the few landing areas in Fiordland, and Bradshaw had landed there numerous times.

At 2.30 p.m. the Fox Moth left Invercargill with four passengers: William Hunt (farmer), Walter Sutton Jones (journalist), George Ross (stock and station agency clerk) and Catherine Buckingham. The first three were bound for Franz Josef, with a stopover at Big Bay to drop off Buckingham and pick up May Robbie.[3]

Davey, Robbie and Marjorie Mehaffey (a surgery attendant)

Arthur Bradshaw (left) with the Fox Moth (SK-ADC) he crashed at Big Bay on 30 December 1936. This photo was taken in September 1935. The passengers about to take a scenic flight over Milford Sound are W. Hunt, J. Wade and T. Carson.

Arthur Bradshaw Collection

had gone ahead of the rest of the tramping party and were waiting near the hut for the plane to arrive. The weather was good and the passengers had a pleasant flight to Big Bay, but as the plane approached the landing area on the beach it stalled and crashed into heavy surf over a metre high. Pilot Bradshaw was thrown out on impact, along with Buckingham, who was badly injured. Hunt and Ross were also thrown from the plane, but each managed to grab hold of a wing as the aircraft wallowed in the surf.[4]

Davey and his companions did not see the crash because their view was blocked by sand dunes, but they had seen the plane begin to fall and raced to the beach. Davey, first on the scene, found Bradshaw, bleeding from a head wound, carrying the injured Buckingham. Davey took over and carried Buckingham up the beach to Robbie. He then ran back to the hut to get a first-aid kit. Robbie made Buckingham as comfortable as possible and went down into the surf to help Bradshaw search for Jones, who was missing. They found him underwater with a severe head wound, and brought him to shore. Robbie, Mehaffey and Bradshaw attempted artificial resuscitation for an hour without success. Jones had probably died instantly from a blow to the left temple. He was only 21.[5]

The remaining passengers were in considerable pain. Buckingham had fractures to her skull, forearm, femur and pelvis, a severe scalp wound and a damaged right eye. Hunt had a fractured vertebra and rib, and Ross had a fractured femur and sternum and a hip injury. Bradshaw had cut hands, a bad cut on his head and a fractured vertebra.

By now the rest of the tramping party had arrived and, using a stretcher that Davey knocked up from wood and flax, carried the injured to Big Bay Hut. Bradshaw recalled that Robbie and Mehaffey did 'magnificent' first-aid work with very little equipment.[6] Robbie used her clothing to stop patients' bleeding, and others gave all their spare clothing to try to keep them warm. They were in shock and Robbie heated and reheated stones and pieces of metal in the fire as a way of providing added warmth.[7]

All the injured required urgent hospital treatment, for which they needed transport. Would the alarm be raised by the hotel at Franz Josef when they failed to turn up? Or would the plane and its passengers not be missed until they failed to return to Invercargill the following evening? It was too long to wait. Davey knew he would have to go for help.

The nearest contact with the outside world was at Marian Corner, 90 kilometres away, where there was a phone at the Public Works Department camp. It would take a very fit tramper three days to get there, but Davey knew he would have to do better than that. Fortunately, he was used to travelling in the dark.

He set off on foot at about 7.30 p.m. This, he decided, would be faster than riding a horse on the slippery rocks. He reached Martins Bay Hut sometime after midnight and stopped

Arthur Bradshaw, about 1939.
Arthur Bradshaw Collection

for a brew and something to eat. Then he got into this dinghy, which, knowing Davey, he probably had to bail out and perhaps even repair. At about 2.30 a.m. he began rowing up Lake McKerrow.[8]

The lake is 15 kilometres long and there was a slight head wind. That, coupled with the fact that Davey had only been able to find oars of different lengths, meant it was going to be a long night. The trip was made more difficult by the fact that Davey had recently dislocated a rib while working in the stockyards at Martins Bay. Every pull on the oars was painful until about halfway up the lake, when he felt the rib click back into place.[9]

He reached the hut near the head of Lake McKerrow at 7.30 a.m. One of the two trampers staying at the hut later described him as looking 'white, weary and worried'. He was only just over halfway to Marian Corner, after nearly 12 hours. The trampers gave Davey a hurried breakfast and he set off on horseback at about 8.30 a.m.[10]

The remaining 40 kilometres of track climbed gently but steadily, particularly from Humboldt Falls (today's road-end) to Marian Corner. Trampers would take about 15 hours to walk the distance, with at least one overnight stop. While the track was reasonable as far as Deadmans Hut, where Davey stopped to rest his horse, it deteriorated after that, and ended abruptly near Sunny Creek, where trampers climbed up to Lake Howden and the Greenstone Valley. The road from Marian Corner down the Hollyford had not yet been formed and Davey had to follow a newly cut survey line. Leaving his horse, he continued on foot, climbing over and around many large

Arthur Bradshaw took this photo of Ernie Clark and Davey Gunn after his first landing at Martins Bay in May 1937. Unfortunately, the riverside strip didn't survive the first flood of the winter.

Arthur Bradshaw Collection

boulders and trees strewn about from when the Milford Road, which runs above the Hollyford at this point, was being formed by dynamite blasting.[11]

He arrived at Marian Corner about 3.30 p.m. – 20 hours after he left Big Bay, having covered the last 40 kilometres in about seven hours. Davey's phone call galvanised the district's rescue services. The Southland Aero Club and Southland Airways each readied a plane for take-off at 4.30 p.m. One carried Dr Lawrence McNickle, superintendent of Southland Hospital. Both planes arrived at Big Bay at about 6 p.m.[12]

Timing was crucial, as the planes had to be back in Southland by 8.30 p.m., the official curfew for small planes. An added complication was that the beach landing area could only be used within two hours either side of low tide. It was a stroke of luck that the tide was low when Davey's message came through, and there was just enough daylight left.

As it turned out, the hotel staff at Franz Josef did not raise the alarm when their booked guests failed to turn up. Ernie Clark, Southland Airways' ground engineer and part-time pilot, had, however, became worried about the non-return of Bradshaw and his passengers. He was about to set off in the company's Puss Moth to search for the missing plane when he received the call to fuel up and prepare to fly to Big Bay.[13] Clark would have had no idea where to start looking on his own, and little chance of finding the plane before dark, let alone rescuing anyone. Without Davey's trip the injured group would certainly have had to spend another night (or more) at Big Bay, which would have been uncomfortable at the least, and possibly disastrous.

Dr McNickle had only an hour to make the patients comfortable for travel before the planes took off again, at about 7 p.m. The first plane carried Buckingham and Hunt, the most seriously injured, and landed at Invercargill about 8.30 p.m. The second aircraft carried Ross and only made it as far as Mossburn before dark. An ambulance was waiting there to take the patient to Southland Hospital. The planes returned the following day to take out McNickle, Bradshaw, and Jones's body.

The people of Southland soon heard about the accident through the local papers. The *Southland Times* account of the accident quoted McNickle on Davey's journey, which was headlined 'An Amazing Feat'. McNickle stated that the journey had

Davey near Long Reef Point only a few hours before the plane crash. The photograph was taken by G. G. Stewart, who was very surprised to see Davey again only 18 hours later at McKerrow Hut on his way to raise the alarm.
Murray Gunn Collection

Davey (centre) with a walking party on Big Bay beach. Planes landed on the beach in the distance.

Isabel Findlay

possibly saved two lives. The paper's reporter had his or her geography a little confused, stating that Davey had 'walked, or rather climbed, the long track across the Main Divide', but nonetheless the people of Southland were impressed:[14]

> Only those who knew the nature of the rough mountain country could appreciate the merit of the trip, and the almost superhuman speed with which it was done, the doctor [McNickle] said. Experienced trampers would regard three days as a very fast time for the trip, but Mr Gunn, who had previously worked untiringly in the rescue of the injured, made it in less than one day.[15]

After raising the alarm Davey, apparently suffering no ill-effects from his journey, headed back into the Hollyford, spending the night of 1 January 1937 at Pyke Hut. En route he heard a plane heading to Big Bay, which must have been gratifying. He himself never recorded an account of the trip. Family friend Ian Speden recounted that Davey would discuss it with close friends, but in public he would brush off questions and refuse to discuss details.[16]

Follow-up articles mostly focused on the inquest for Jones. On 15 January the *Southland Times* published a letter from 'Admirer', suggesting that Davey's journey should not be forgotten and that perhaps the paper could invite donations to commemorate it: 'Besides a presentation to Mr Gunn, it might be appropriate to erect a small cairn at the spot where Mr Gunn arrived at the road.' An editorial in the same edition endorsed the sentiments of its correspondent and invited 'subscriptions' together with suggestions on what form the commemoration should take.[17]

Lists of donations received appeared and over the next two weeks, and more than £73 was raised. The editor formed a committee with Walter Jones (father of Walter Sutton Jones and editor of the *Southland Daily News*), Dr Lawrence McNickle and David Jennings (president of the Southland branch of the New Zealand Alpine Club). The committee announced its decision to use a small portion of the money to erect a permanent commemoration of Davey's feat, at the point where he reached the Hollyford Road. The rest of the money would be given to Davey. Davey wrote thanking the subscribers, and announced that he hoped to use the money to install a radio transmitter at Martins Bay or to improve the accommodation at Big Bay.[18]

An official inquiry into the cause of the crash was held

Below left: Davey's hut at Big Bay, where nurse May Robbie and fellow trampers cared for those injured in the plane crash.

Below: The fireplace on which May Robbie heated stones and pieces of metal in order to keep her patients warm and ward off shock.

Eric Midgley

Subscription List[24]

	£ s d		£ s d
The Southland Times Co.	2 2 0	G. Ross	1 1 0
Dr L. C. McNickle	1 1 0	B. B. J.	1 0 0
Abraham Wachner	1 0 0	Tuatapere Admirer	10 0
W. J. Jones	5 0 0	B. W. and B. M.	5 0
J. S. Baxter	1 0 0	Dr Stanley Brown	1 1 0
R. T. Barnett	10 0	X	5 0
Anonymous	5 0	A. H.	5 0
Well-wisher	5 0	'Scottie'	1 0 0
Rucsac	2 6	Appreciative	5 0
Sir Robert Anderson	2 2 0	Staff St Helen's Hospital	1 0 0
A Londoner	2 2 0	Ivon V. Wilson	1 1 0
In Memoriam – W. S. J.	1 1 0	Archdeacon J. A. and Mrs Lush	2 0 0
Admirer	5 0	Munro Boys and Susie	1 1 0
Anonymous	5 0	Tramper	3 6
Dr David Jennings	1 1 0	Two Trampers	2 6
J. B. Thomson	2 2 0	James Holland	1 10 0
Bluff Admirer	2 6	Dr R. H. Howells	1 1 0
O. H.	5 0	Dr C. C. Anderson	1 1 0
W. G. Tait	1 1 0	Hiker	2 6
Invercargill Fire Brigade	1 1 0	Dunedin Supporter	1 1 0
W. Thompson	1 1 0	Margaret Cecilia	5 0
A. B. Macalister	1 1 0	Mrs C. J. Broderick	2 2 0
A. J. Hawke	1 1 0	R. W.	10 6
Eustace Russell	1 1 0	Two Scouts	5 0
D. Cuthbertson	1 1 0	Two Well-Wishers	10 0
C. G.	1 1 0	W. J. A. M.	1 1 0
Rubai'yat	10 0	Dunedinite	2 6
Backblocks	1 0 0	One Who Knows	2 6
D. P.	1 1 0	J. C.	2 0
A Poor Man's Mite	2 0 0	J. A.	2 0
John Macdonald	1 1 0	Stiffy	2 0
X	2 6	J. S.	2 0
M. H.	3 0	J. T. Carswell	1 0 0
House Surgeons, Public Hospital	1 1 0	Staff Carswell and Co. Ltd	15 0
I. Copeland	1 1 0	Tim Doolan	10 0
Admirer No. 2	5 0	J. B. Reid	1 1 0
Two Sympathizers	5 0	Members Invercargill Police Force	1 1 0
M. N. Hyndman	2 2 0	Staff of Herbert Haynes Ltd	3 4 0
W. B.	1 1 0	Admirer	2 6
Alex Stewart (Balfour)	1 0 0	J. S. Marshall	1 1 0
Staff, Vacuum Oil Company	10 0	Texas Co. Employees	10 0
W. S. Todd	1 1 0	TOTAL	73 17 6

over the winter of 1937 and Bradshaw was charged with fail-
ing to ensure that the plane was satisfactorily loaded, exceed-
ing the maximum permissible load, and using an unlicensed
landing ground. The second charge was dismissed because no
one could establish what load the plane had been carrying, but
Bradshaw was convicted on the other two charges. The magis-
trate stated that every person and piece of baggage should have
been weighed. However, he also praised Bradshaw for showing 'great courage at the time of the accident characteristic of
the true British pioneering spirit'.[19] Bradshaw appealed against
the convictions, and the charge of using an unlicensed landing
ground was quashed.[20]

In May 1937 Davey was awarded a Coronation Medal for
his part in the Big Bay rescue. Some 90,000 of these medals
were struck 'for issue as a personal souvenir from his Majesty
[King George VI] to persons in Crown services and others in
the United Kingdom and in other parts of the Empire'. More
than 1,200 medals were awarded in New Zealand. Davey also
received a citation, and both were later passed on to his son
Murray, but were unfortunately lost when Murray's museum at
Hollyford Camp burned down in February 1990.[21]

The actions of May Robbie received less public recognition, but a meeting of the Invercargill nursing division of the
St John Ambulance Brigade passed a minute of appreciation

Davey rowed to the head
of Lake McKerrow in a
dinghy like this. He is here
pictured at the oars with
Ruth Benstead and an
unknown man.

Murray Gunn Collection

The memorial stone laid at Marian Corner in recognition of Davey's efforts.

of her services, and an article repeating Dr H. Gibson's praise of her actions appeared in the *Southland Times*. Robbie later nursed in London, became matron of Whangarei Hospital, and owned a private hospital for the aged in Christchurch. She died in Christchurch in 1965. Arthur Bradshaw went on to have a notable flying career that included service with the RNZAF and RAF during World War Two. Catherine Buckingham recovered and continued with her nursing career, becoming matron at Wanganui Hospital. She died in Wanganui in 1989, aged 90.[22]

A monument was erected at Marian Corner within a year or two of the accident, and this is still viewed by tourists today. Davey joked rather prophetically that the memorial was his tombstone. The rest of the money raised must have been a welcome contribution to Davey's coffers. He was also presented with a gold watch, which he kept in a cupboard at Deadmans Hut. Many years later the watch was stolen from Murray Gunn's museum.[23]

Chapter Five

Mustering the Hollyford

He was twice alive when he was after cattle.[1]

After the plane crash at Big Bay, Davey's name became widely known by the people of Southland. Subsequent articles about the trips he ran in the area meant he also became celebrated in tramping and climbing circles throughout New Zealand.[2] But despite the publicity, and the increasing popularity of the Hollyford, Davey's life continued to revolve around his twice-yearly cattle musters. He loved the challenge and found it great sport. It was on a par with big-game hunting – more exciting, he said, than deer stalking or pig hunting.[3] Usually a quiet man, Davey was completely different when chasing cattle:

> He was twice alive when he was after cattle. He was 'Clancy of the Overflow,' he was a joyous 'whistling cowboy,' he had an eye like a hawk ... Davey's 'Way, Leggo Bob,' 'Way Tim,' and 'Out Black!', his shrill whistles, his ringing 'ho-ho' to the cattle, and less mild and more reasonable original language galvanised the muster.[4]

A muster could take anywhere from two to four months, and the men would travel about 200 kilometres along the valleys and coastline searching for cattle in the bush and clearings. Because the bush was dense, the musterers stuck to the open country and used their dogs to find the cattle:

> The procedure was simply to set the dogs alight into the bush every now and then in the hope that they'd find something. Davey Gunn's dogs became particularly good at this. He would simply say 'Seek!' and away they'd go. If they

Davey in his element, taking a break while mustering cattle near Hokuri River.
Murray Gunn Collection

Packhorses and musterers crossing Hidden Falls Creek, about 1954. Jack Jenkins (left) and Jean Prust.

Ed Cotter

found nothing they'd come back after having scouted about for a mile or so and the procedure would be repeated a bit further on. It was a slow process and pretty hard on dogs.[5]

It could be pretty hard on humans, too. Working in the bush on foot with wild cattle was dangerous. Davey was charged quite often by angry beasts but took this in his stride, as one of his musterers recalled:

> Any one of the adventures and escapes Dave had, which he dismissed as mere incidents in a day's work, would serve most men as a tale to be told for a lifetime! One night we were undressing and I noticed a huge bruise on the inside of this thigh and remarked on it. Dave said laconically, 'That old cow hooked me and chucked me into the bush.'[6]

The autumn muster (February to April) consisted of finding cattle in the Martins Bay, Hokuri and Kaipo areas, and castrating or marking them as necessary. It was easy to miss a few, and quite often two- or three-year-old animals would be found with no marking. Some of the cattle would then be taken into the Pyke Valley (Barrier and Alabaster areas) to winter over. In the spring muster (October to December) Martins Bay and the Pyke Valley would be covered again, and about a hundred cattle would be selected for sale and driven out to the market.[7]

It took two days to prepare for the start of each muster. Provisions were packed into wheat sacks to be loaded onto packhorses. Supplies included flour, sugar, oatmeal, potatoes, cheese, bacon, dried fruit, tea, butter, jam, milk powder and tins of meat.[8] Numerous people recorded Davey's fondness for pea-meal, which he used for soups and as a thickener, and plenty of this would be included in the provisions. The staple diet for the dogs was meat-meal. Davey would boil this with pollard (a by-product of flour milling) until it was a very thick paste. When this mixture cooled it would be doled out in big chunks, which the dogs loved.[9]

Davey would check the condition of the horses and fix new shoes if required. Equipment for the muster included rifles, axes, rope, files, slashers, staples and shoeing gear. Personal gear was added on the day of departure, and when everything was ready the dogs would be released. For a while there would be pande-monium as the excited dogs raced around barking gleefully.[10]

In the early days travelling with the dogs was relatively straightforward, but from the late 1930s the area became home to hundreds (and later thousands) of deer. The dogs could not resist and would take off as a pack when they smelt their prey:

> Davey was often given dogs by people who found them too rough on sheep. Despite behaving with utmost friend-liness around a camp they worked like a pack of hungry wolves. When they got onto a deer they were off and noth-ing would stop them. All Davey could do was to go to the nearest hut and wait for them to turn up, which might take a couple of days.[11]

Davey (standing, left) with trampers outside his hut in the Kaipo Valley.
Gordon Speden Collection

Once the deer became numerous Davey would send one of his men on ahead of the main party to shoot any of these animals that were near the track, or at least scare them away from where the dogs might smell them.

The party of musterers, horses and dogs would aim to make it from Deadmans to Pyke Hut on the first night. On arrival at a hut there was wood to chop, dogs to feed and the evening meal to prepare. Musterer Rupert Sharpe recalled that Davey was a good cook. 'Every evening we had pea soup nearly as thick as porridge, a slab of deer meat and potatoes. A man doesn't need much more than that.'[12]

Derek Turnbull also had fond memories of the food: 'We'd have venison, a lot of tinned stuff, milk powder and a luxury was eggs. Eggs were wrapped in newspaper and packed in a biscuit tin . . . Also semolina and rice, that kind of thing. It was good tucker.'[13]

Davey prided himself on his porridge and would soak the oats overnight. He had a special spoon (which he called a spirtle) at each hut and would patiently stir the mixture until it boiled. After the porridge there would be bacon, which Davey reckoned

Jack Jenkins with cattle in the Kaipo Valley.
Ed Cotter

Working a mob of cattle at Martins Bay.

Ed Cotter

filled the men up for longer than other meats. Or, as he would say, 'It stood to one better.'[14]

The second day, weather and dogs permitting, the mustering party would try to make it all the way to Martins Bay. A rowboat would be used to take the stores and gear down Lake McKerrow while one or two of the men took the dogs and horses around the side of the lake – on the 'Demon Trail'.

Once at Martins Bay one of the first jobs was to get together a small mob of cattle from the flats around the hut. They would be put into a paddock and 'worked' for a while to quieten them, before being taken out and used as a decoy mob to encourage other cattle to come out of the bush. The men would hold the decoy mob while Davey and his dogs entered the bush. Rupert Sharpe, who worked on a muster in 1949, wrote a lovely description of the first day at Martins Bay. Davey had sent his dogs into the bush after cattle and suddenly there was a lot of barking:

> 'You two stay here and hold the decoys,' he told us. 'I'll go in and try to hunt this lot out onto the shingle.'
>
> Tying his horse at the edge of the bush, Gunn disappeared. It looked to me as if the bail-up was about ten chains in from the forest fringe, and I didn't see how any man on foot could steer cattle through that sort of bush.
>
> 'How the hell will he get them out?' I asked Jim [Sinclair].

A mob of decoy cattle being driven up the Kaipo River.
Ed Cotter

'There's a lot of luck in it,' he replied. 'Dave will work his way round behind them, and when he's in position he'll call the dogs off and let the beasts see him. When they see a man on foot they spook mighty easy, and when they see Dave they'll make a break. If we're lucky, and Dave can keep the dogs from stopping them, they'll break right out into the open and maybe run into this mob.'

. . . All we could hear was the barking of dogs . . . After about half an hour we heard Dave calling his dogs away from the cattle in the bush. Unlike the high country musterer, who can make his dogs hear him at a range of a mile or more, Gunn had a very quiet voice. His dog work was all done at close range, and he had no reason to bellow. For a minute or two there was dead silence. Then, as the cattle sighted or smelt old Dave, they bolted, with a crashing and smashing which would have done credit to a herd of elephants. Within seconds the dogs resumed their chorus.

'Must have gone the wrong way.' said Jim. 'Dave's stopping them with the dogs so that he can give them a fresh start.'

This sort of thing went on for the best part of an hour. At intervals Jim and I moved our few cattle to some other point in the clearing, which might be nearer the periodic uproar that showed us where Gunn and his suite were in action . . . Eventually we caught a glimpse of the red and white of a big Hereford beast as it charged along the edge of the bush, and the next bail-up occurred in a tongue of bush which reached out into the clearing . . .

'We'll get those cattle now,' said Sinclair. 'You watch this mob and I'll go in and tell Dave where they are. In the bush you can't always see which way to start them.'

Circling slowly around the decoys, I let them drift close to the point of the tongue of bush, in which the barking dogs and an occasional snort told of the proximity of the quarry . . . After many more minutes I heard Gunn and Sinclair talking loudly, to make it clear to the suspicious beasts ahead that their line of retreat was well blocked, and suddenly two big Hereford bulls burst into the open and trotted towards the decoys. Three old cows followed them, and that was the lot.

Without calves to defend, against dogs ready and well able to pull down a young beast and kill it, these older cattle were equally well able to defend themselves, and to my surprise they were scarcely out of breath. Nor was Gunn, when he presently came out of the bush. Unless a beast was

Jack Jenkins in the cattle yards at Martins Bay.
Ed Cotter

chasing him he moved at his own pace, which was not fast, and to him this sort of work was just routine.

'Got them without much trouble,' he observed ... If we had got these 'without much trouble' the job had still taken the best part of an afternoon, and it dawned on me that what Dave called 'trouble' would be worth watching.[15]

From Davey's hut at Martins Bay the men would then head across the river to the flats near the old McKenzie homestead, which was known simply as McKenzies. Cattle grazing in that area would be mustered and put into holding paddocks and the calves marked. Then the team would head down the coast with a decoy mob to muster cattle at the Kaipo River. Cattle grazed up the river as far as the flats at the head of the valley, and it took two or three days to find them and bring them in. The cattle here were relatively wild (compared with Davey's 'tame' cattle), as they had no contact with men or dogs between musters. Derek Turnbull noted some fine specimens: 'Davey kept bulls around there [Kaipo]. The old bulls just died of old age. Some of them were tremendous, they'd leave hoofprints like elephants!'[16]

Once they had found all the cattle they could, the men would drive the mob down the valley and back along the coast to McKenzies. Getting the sale cattle across the Hollyford River was another adventure, according to Ed Cotter:

The way to do it was to go up to the mouth of the lagoon, cross it and then continue up the river until you were oppo-site the hut. Then you would stampede them into the river. They'd cross and come out at various points downstream from there.[17]

The cattle were reluctant to enter the water, but Davey found that 'if you put a wall of dogs behind them they would start to swim, after a while'.[18]

During one crossing the cattle panicked when the man in the dinghy stationed upstream (to make sure they didn't swim the wrong way) inadvertently got the boat in among the cattle. Some reached the far shore but most turned back. Davey collec-ted them up, calmed them down and made another attempt to cross, this time using just a downstream dinghy. This was not entirely successful. Further attempts followed but, come night-fall, there were still two steers left to cross.

'Persuading' cattle to ford the
Pyke River.
Ed Cotter

The next day, when the tide was high, Davey tried once more to drive the two steers into the river. But they were determined not to cross, and they could swim faster than Davey's horse could move to stop them coming back out. A decoy mob placed on the opposite riverbank did not interest them, so Davey lassoed them and tried to pull them across behind the dinghy. That didn't work either. With his dogs and horses exhausted from working in deep water, Davey stopped and had the steers taken back to the yards.

Anyone else would have given up at this point and left the two steers in peace until the next muster, but not Davey Gunn. The next morning he had those steers back at the river and battle recommenced. One of them charged his horse and gored it slightly. While Davey was waiting for his .303 to be brought over so he could shoot the beast's horns off he decided to try just once again. He pacified the steers and drove them down to the river. This time they simply swam calmly across to the decoy mob. Davey had finally worn down their resistance. It had taken the best part of two and a half days, but Davey was satisfied.[19]

Cattle on the way from the Kaipo to Martins Bay.
Ed Cotter

Once all the wet cattle had been collected up from wherever they had landed on the riverbank they would be added to the mob already at Martins Bay. Then it was time to draft the cattle again, earmark and castrate the calves and sort out some sale cattle. If a beast was very difficult to handle, Davey would remove its horns. He had a pair of cattle dehorners, but they were heavy and awkward to carry, so once the animal was in the crush he would usually either knock the horns off with a heavy stick or shoot them off with his .303.[20]

Davey did not hold with new technology, and even castrating calves was done with a basic implement:

> Some of them [cattle] were really big and really wild. Davey had this rickety old but workable crush and we'd eventually get the animal in there. My job was to get the rail in there so they couldn't back out. Then Davey would stand there in

the crush behind the animal and say, 'Pass me the machine' and I'd pass him his pocketknife. He was down there [in the Hollyford] to get away from the machine age and even a pocketknife was a piece of machinery.[21]

Rupert Sharpe well remembered the dangers of being on foot in a yard with semi-wild cattle. Each man, he said, was armed with a manuka pole that could be used on any beast that attempted to charge.[22] Some found the experience somewhat disconcerting, but not Davey, who had almost no fear when it came to cattle, as Gordon Donaldson–Law observed: 'Working in the corralls is a gory, and at times exciting job, and it is well to work with an eye on the fence. More than once I saw a cow go at Dave who stood his ground and kicked her on the nose!'[23]

The team would spend a few days finding cattle in the Hokuri Creek area before leaving Martins Bay for Big Bay with their mob of sale cattle. The route followed the coast for the entire 17 kilometres, and the usual practice was to have one man leading the mob and another following behind. Sometimes the trip to Big Bay would be uneventful, but cattle would often try to escape into the bush or turn back the way they had come, meaning many frustrating hours trying to recover them:[24]

> That was always hectic, trying to keep the cattle in line. Occasionally one would head off into the scrub. We had one person at the front and one at the back and often we would find that we only had half a herd, and that the others had all sneaked off somewhere.[25]

The yards at Big Bay, with Joan Speden in the foreground.

Gordon Speden Collection

Donaldson-Law wrote of a mob of 40 cattle being broken up by Davey's dogs chasing a deer right through the middle of them. The musterers were left with only the five leading cattle.[26] Such a disruption could result in hours (or days) searching for cattle in the bush and persuading them to rejoin what remained of the mob.

At Big Bay a few days might be spent mustering any cattle that were about, repairing the yards and clearing the track through to the Pyke Valley for the next stage. The routine was repeated at the Upper Pyke, where one fence posed a particular challenge.

> That fence! I named it 'Dave's Folly', though in fairness to Dave, I believe that the McKenzies were to blame for it. Anyway, many years ago . . . someone wanting a fence and lacking wire, felled a line of trees, filling the gaps with saplings and branches. It wiggle-waggled, over gullies, through a marsh, and along the top of a high bank for about a quarter of a mile. When not in use the deer make gaps in it and before it can be used these gaps have to be filled. For years trees have been felled on top of trees, branches have been piled on branches. Much of the timber is rotten and nothing, now, could make it secure. For two days we laboured on that mass of futility, where a couple of strands of wire and some posts would have done the job with only a couple of hours attention a year.[27]

Cattle on the road between Deadmans and Marian Corner.

Murray Gunn Collection

Jack Jenkins with cattle at the head of Lake Alabaster.
Ed Cotter

From the Upper Pyke a day or two would be spent mustering the upper flats before men and cattle went down to the hut at the Barrier River. There they again mended fences, and mustered the Pyke Valley flats as well as the Diorite and Olivine areas. If it was the autumn muster, a mob of cattle would be taken up into the Barrier Valley to winter over. In the spring the men would bring the cattle down the Pyke Valley:

> Coming around the lakes, Wilmot and Alabaster, was always quite a difficult part of the trip. Dave or someone earlier had blasted the track and the cliff faces, particularly around Wilmot, usually needed to be cleared and that caused a day or two's delay.[28]

Other hazards could also slow the muster at this point, as Davey's friend Jean Prust recorded:

> Droving on the bush tracks took time . . . Often they [the cattle] would 'string out' and even stop altogether and dogs would be sent 'out' to persuade them to move on again. Over the narrow parts of the bluff track they would 'bunch' and jostle each other and frequently one or two would fall over the edge, thus necessitating their rescue by bringing

them back to the mob via a suitable gradient up the bluff side and sometimes a track would have to be cleared to do this.'[29]

Before deer began to eat out the areas that provided feed for cattle in the Lower Pyke and at Hidden Falls, Davey kept cattle there, and these would have to be mustered as well. From Hidden Falls the cattle were taken out to Deadmans, and sometimes that could be a long day:

> We did not get a start with them [the cattle] until after lunch next day – you know how Dave likes to work in the cool of the evening – and about 3 o'clock heavy rain fell. When it became dark, we were still in the bush, and, of course, we could see nothing. Leading the packhorse, I was in front, lying flat in the saddle to dodge branches. Every now and then old Dave would sing out from the tail of the mob. Because he seemed to be getting very close to me, I called back to ask whether he could see the cattle which were supposed to be between us. He roared back that everything was all right. When we reached the road near Deadmans, Dave was right behind me and we had no cattle. As luck would have it, we found the mob next day, back at Hidden Falls, and drove it to the road in daylight.[30]

Before the Te Anau–Milford road reached the Hollyford in the late 1930s Davey took his cattle to market the same way as the McKenzies had done: up Pass Creek, over the Greenstone Saddle and down the Greenstone Valley. Sometimes he arranged to meet his friend George Shaw (of Elfin Bay Station) with his sale cattle in the Greenstone Valley, and the pair would join forces and drive their cattle out together. They were great friends but not ideal travelling companions, as Jean Prust observed:

> Davey always travelled light and did not mind if or when he ate, but George liked his food. Once when they reached Mossburn George complained how hungry he was, as 'they had only had some very dry bread for the past two days.' A friend said, 'Davey looks all right, how did he manage?' 'Oh,' said George, 'Davey's got crocodile's teeth, he can eat anything.'[31]

From the Greenstone Valley the route was up the Pass Burn and down the Mavora River to Mavora Lakes, then down the Oreti River to Centre Hill, down the road to Mossburn and on to the saleyards at Lorneville, near Invercargill. Farmers along the way always gave them a paddock to put their cattle in overnight.[32] The trip from the Greenstone to Lorneville would take about nine days, and often Davey's friends would be there at the saleyards to meet him. Although he drank only rarely at home, he liked to have a drink when he was 'out' and would occasionally drink too much whisky when catching up with friends.[33]

After the road reached the upper Hollyford Valley, Davey found it easier to carry on straight up the valley to Marian Corner. From there he could take the new road. On this route the first night after leaving Deadmans was spent at Cascade Creek. There was no paddock there, so the drovers took it in turns to watch the cattle during the night. Usually the animals were so tired there was no problem, but Jim Speden told of one time when an electrical storm wrought havoc: 'Every now and then I would start after a beast who seemed to be away from

Davey (right) with cattle outside Hidden Falls Hut, 1950.

Gordon Speden Collection

Kaipo cattle on the beach at
Martins Bay.

Ed Cotter

the rest and it would turn out to be Dave, and every now and
then I would find him trying to work my horse back into the
mob.'[34]

The next night would be spent in the Eglinton Valley and
the following day the first of the stations would be reached – Te
Anau Downs, owned by the Chartres family. Davey and Johnny
Chartres were good friends, and sometimes Chartres would ride
out to meet Davey and camp with the musterers in the Eglinton
Valley. Ed Cotter recalled one such occasion:

> Once the cattle were settled down for the night they
> wouldn't move . . . Johnny brought out a bottle of whisky.
> 'Have some whisky.' 'Thank you,' says Dave and we had
> a few whiskies. The next night Davey got out the [same]
> whisky bottle and said, 'Have one on us tonight, Johnny,'
> as though it was his bottle of whisky![35]

When the drovers reached Te Anau Downs Station they
would have a day off, with the cattle grazing in one of Chartres's
grassy paddocks. The dogs also needed a rest after walking along
miles and miles of shingle road, which was much harder on
their paws than the bush tracks they were used to.[36]

From Te Anau Downs it was on to Linwood Station, then Burwood, Centre Hill and Mossburn. 'That's the part my father loved, doing the muster,' said son Murray. 'Driving the cattle along the road and meeting his friends along the way.'[37] The cattle needed a long rest around midday to eat and drink enough for the extended journey, so they covered only about 16 kilometres a day. Davey enjoyed chatting to the people he encountered along the way, and preferred to walk behind the mob, only riding his horse to do the morning and evening head-counts. Sometimes he trucked his cattle to Lorneville from Mossburn, but usually he drove them there himself, staying along the way with friends such as Andrew Chartres at Murray Creek, Bill Harrison at Dipton, Mr Smith at Forty Trees and Mr Duthie at Lochiel.

By the time they reached the saleyards the cattle had lost condition – the Kaipo cattle had walked the furthest: some 340 kilometres – and consequently they did not fetch the highest prices.[38] Some might have thought it was scarcely worth all the effort, but it was the proceeds of these sales that allowed Davey to carry on living in the Hollyford, so he was happy. And in time his cattle became prized by some:

> Davey would only bring out about 100 cattle a year and in those days I think they might have averaged about £30. So he would make about £3,000, which was quite a lot of money in those days. There were always some big Herefords among them and some people bought them year after year. They were tremendous cattle once you fattened them up a bit. The cattle were well civilised by the time they got to the sales.[39]

Chapter Six

Davey's Companions

He was hard on horses but he kissed his dogs.[1]

Davey's mustering operation relied heavily on his horses and his dogs. The horses had to be multi-skilled: quiet enough to be used on the guided treks, strong and agile enough to pack stores over rough tracks, and obedient and fast enough for the dangerous work of mustering.

They tended to be short and stocky with heavy legs, and looked a bit like miniature draughthorses. Many were bred from a black half-Arab stallion called Balls, which was based at Martins Bay before World War Two. If any women asked its name Davey would always find some way of avoiding telling them. After the war Davey unintentionally acquired another sire. Mary Hunt, the daughter of William Hunt who had been injured in the plane crash at Big Bay in 1936, visited Martins Bay on her pony stallion, which she ended up leaving behind. Davey thought it was too small to mount any of the mares, so he left it down there, where it managed to impregnate quite a few. One was Trixie (who had been sired by Balls), who was old and swaybacked, but who had a beautiful foal that was named Thunder.[2]

It was hard country for horses. While the terrain wasn't steep, it was often slippery or boggy. Sandflies were a perennial nuisance and most of the horses learned to stand with their heads in a bush to avoid the worst of them.

Imagine how difficult it must have been for Storm, who, before he came to the Hollyford, had pulled a milk-cart around the flat streets of Invercargill. His tail had been cropped, so his first months in the Hollyford must have been made miserable by

Davey Gunn with devoted friends at Deadmans.
Murray Gunn Collection

Murray Gunn with Storm
(left) and Calm, near
Jamestown, 1953.
Peter Robson

insects. He was a very strong horse but never got used to crossing creeks and was inclined to panic.

The tracks around the bluffs were difficult and one of the
best packhorses, Homer, lost her footing around the side of
Lake Wilmot and fell to her death. All the horses would try
to avoid being taken down the 'Demon Trail' alongside Lake
McKerrow. Given half a chance, they would try to double back
or escape, sometimes by swimming in the lake, which of course
soaked the packed loads.[3]

Swamps presented their own difficulties, as musterer Gordon
Donaldson-Law recalled:

> . . . the trail consisted of a corduroy of loose logs, that rolled
> under the horses feet. English horses would have broken
> their legs in the first few minutes, but these hardy horses, stag-
> gering and stumbling, their hooves squelching and sucking
> in the ooze between the logs, carried us through.[4]

The horses became good at finding their way around the
district, even in the dark. When travelling at night, Davey would

simply lie along the horse's back, not even touching the bridle. When the horse stopped he knew he had arrived at the next hut.[5]

Ed Cotter was impressed at the horses' nocturnal abilities:

> I can remember on one occasion arriving at the end of the lake after dark, I was riding Charlie and suddenly he stopped and just wouldn't go. It was pitch black and I thought, oh, he's tired. It turned out there was a huge tree right across the track. It took ages to find a way around it, because there were saplings everywhere and I couldn't see. When we finally got around Charlie took me to the hut.[6]

Some of the horses, such as Trixie and Kim, could find their own way back to the Hollyford from Southland, and Davey would turn them loose at Dipton when they had finished their cattle-droving duties. On one occasion Trixie failed to arrive home but Davey, knowing there had been a big slip near Lake Howden, sent the men up to look for her and they found her grazing on the flats on the other side of the slip. She was happy to take the track they cleared through the slip and follow them home.[7]

Surprise gained her name from her unexpected arrival. Her mother was living alone at Hidden Falls and must have travelled some distance to find a stallion. Donaldson-Law described Surprise as 'the most cunning and laziest little blackguard of a pony I ever knew'.[8] Another horse, Calm, was a universal favourite, as Rupert Sharpe recalled:

Davey with Trixie.
Gordon Speden Collection

Calm was the quietest mare I ever met. At any halt for lunch she used to lie down, fold her legs beneath her, close her eyes and go to sleep. There was always so much gear on the saddle that she had no chance to roll on it or even flop over on her side. This was just as well, for the man who rode Calm had to carry the gelignite.[9]

Whenever Davey came to a patch of dry-looking scrub he would usually toss a match into it in an effort to keep his clearings from growing over. One day he was walking along at the head of Lake Wilmot with Calm, who was following on behind carrying saddlebags. He saw a likely-looking clump of dry tutu and tossed a match into it. Calm came to the burning bushes, stopped and looked at them, then walked past. Davey glanced back and saw that one of the saddlebags was ablaze. He hurried to beat the fire out. Calm might have been quite unperturbed, but Davey knew that her saddlebags held a box of gelignite, while in the kitbag was a tin of detonators.[10]

Many people commented on the fact that while Davey was not actually cruel to his horses, he did expect a great deal from them. He expected them to carry heavy loads and was quick to punish them if they misbehaved:

I thought he was hard on horses. He overloaded and he didn't shoe as often as he should. That was just the way he was. He was from a different generation and they were harder on horses. But it wasn't deliberate and it wasn't crippling them or anything.[11]

Murray Gunn remembered Calm as an old mare. '[She] was gone in the front legs. The poor old thing had trouble walking downhill but he thrashed her along.'[12]

Davey's horses were tough, which was just as well:

No horses, except those actually bred in the bush, could face up to the hardships that fall to their lot. They have to hop from root to root on bush tracks, or from boulder to boulder on the lake-shore – for all the world like mountain goats. During a muster they must do this for ten or twelve hours a day, often for months on end, with hardly a day off.[13]

One of Davey's teenage helpers, Alan Snook, had a theory about why Davey was hard on his horses: 'It was because he

Davey on Surprise.
Murray Gunn Collection

Davey and friends.
Derek and Pat Turnbull Collection

could do without them. He could walk the legs off anyone – he was a very fast walker. But he couldn't do without his dogs. He couldn't find cattle without them.'[14]

Davey loved his dogs and they loved him. There are very few photos of him that don't show him being shadowed by at least one of his faithful admirers. Mostly border collies and bull terriers, each had it individual specialty. Some were finders. Travelling along with the musterers, Davey would see marks in the mud. He would look at them and say something like, 'They must be about two-year-olds and there are probably about 12 of them.' At a particular whistle, four or five finders would take off looking for the cattle. Sometimes they would be gone for ages, but once they found cattle they would start barking and the rest of the dogs would take off to join them. The musterers would tie their horses at the edge of the bush and walk in to where the dogs had the cattle bailed up, then drive them out into a clearing.[15]

Rock, a big black and white dog, never seemed to do any-thing except follow Davey around. One day Alan Snook said to him, 'I don't know why you bother feeding that dog – it never does anything.' 'You'll see,' said Davey. 'You'll see.' When the pair took a mob of cattle to the saleyards they camped for a night in the Greenstone Valley. Alan woke during the night to find that Rock was guarding the cattle and would snap at any cow that tried to wander away in the darkness. Another dog, Rum, had the job of going ahead and clearing local cattle off the route Davey was taking through the runholder's land.[16]

The dogs were mostly fed on meat-meal and, in latter years, ate plenty of venison, but they also had more unorthodox fare. Every two months or so Davey and one of his workers would go down to Lake Alabaster and catch a lot of eels, which they boiled up in a 44-gallon drum. When these had cooled they would be fed to the dogs – Alan Snook said this gave them a wonderful glossy coat.[17] It was also said that they were occasionally fed on trout. Davey would share any leftovers with his dogs, including his porridge. Nothing was too good for them. Big Bay visitor Daphne Midgley remembers the whitebaiters telling her that Davey shared with his dogs, but she didn't believe it until she saw him cleaning the excess porridge out of the pot one morning. He would take one spoonful for himself, then give a dog a full spoon, then take another spoonful himself.[18]

Rupert Sharpe admired Davey for the care he gave his dogs – 'far better care than they would have received on plenty of prosperous farms in more accessible regions'.[19]

Derek Turnbull recalled that 'Davey always had a great collection of dogs, usually dogs that nobody else could handle and sometimes the men were the same'.[20]

The declaration of war in September 1939 and the start of voluntary enlistment meant that Davey began to experience difficulties finding men to work for him. Young, fit men were in short supply. For the first part of the war Hugh McKenzie worked for Davey as a musterer. In 1940 Davey was fortunate enough to find Bill Norman, who stayed with him for most of the rest of the war years. During the summer school holidays the young sons of family friends such as the Turnbulls also came in to help out.[21]

Bill Brown, whose father, Norman, was a good friend of Davey's, went back to the Hollyford for the summer with Davey in 1944. He was only 10 and initially found it a rather strange and frightening experience. The pair were dropped by bus at Marian Corner in the early evening and spent some time organising the horses and packing stores before setting off down the valley. By the time they came to cross the Hollyford to reach Deadmans, it was dark and the river was high, but they made it safely.

Hugh McKenzie, who worked as a musterer for Davey during World War Two.
Isabel Findlay

Once they went to bed Bill found that Davey apparently had terrible nightmares and would roar out in his sleep. He also seemed to be trying to work his dogs. Bill was horrified and initially wanted to go home, but he ended up staying for six weeks, and returned the following two summers. When he was 12 he guided a tramping party of Hawke's Bay students for Davey and remembered that some of the students' songs 'were a bit rough'. Today it seems astonishing that a 12-year-old would be entrusted with the care of a tramping party, but Davey obviously thought Bill was up to the job.[22]

Another summer companion during the war years (and after) was Ruth Benstead, a physical education teacher from Christchurch. Born in England, Ruth had come to New Zealand as a child with her parents, George and Grace, in 1908. Both were teachers at Campbell Park School at Otekaike, George being principal. Ruth herself trained as a teacher. A 1937 photo shows her as part of a tramping party (which included author Elsie K. Morton) in the Hollyford, and this is presumably when she met Davey. He seems to have been attractive to women, and Ian Speden suggested that this was partly because of his quiet, considered, gentlemanly nature – and his uniqueness. Certainly his lifestyle would have been extremely attractive to a fit, hardy woman used to working to a timetable.[23]

Gordon Speden (left) with Davey and the packhorse called Homer, 1948.

Gordon Speden Collection

Alan Snook with Rock, Meg, Help, Rum, Bess and Sharp, about 1940.

Derek and Pat Turnbull Collection

Ruth Benstead was a pleasant, adventurous, determined woman in her mid-thirties when she met Davey. She was very fit and independent, and exuded an air of being 'quite capable of looking after herself', which, Speden said, made her a little bit unusual in the 1940s. She became great friends with Speden's parents, Gordon and Emma, in Gore, and in December 1943 she took their son Ian down the Hollyford. He remembers that Ruth and Davey were 'close friends' by then and that Ruth spent every summer holiday in the Hollyford until her place was usurped by Jean Prust in the early 1950s.[24]

By the late 1930s Davey had learned a lot about the country he lived in. He had sorted out what timbers were good for what. His favourite firewood for making bread was broadleaf, and he always made sure there was a good supply at every hut. When Alan Snook badly cut his hand with a slasher, Davey covered the wound with the gel found at the base of flax leaves and then used a flax leaf to bind up the hand, telling Alan not to take it off until it fell off. Alan said the wound healed well, with no scar. Considering Davey had nearly lost his own hand in a similar incident 10 years earlier, this was a brave form of treatment that he was obviously confident would work.[25]

During the war the Public Works Department camp known as Hendersons Camp (about six kilometres up the road from Deadmans) was empty so Davey got his stores delivered there. In mid-December 1939 he and Alan Snook began the job of

Ruth Benstead (on the right in the dinghy) and friends, including Elsie K. Morton (sitting next to Ruth), at Martins Bay.

Murray Gunn Collection

packing stores down the valley. Davey had a fairly new horse called Willie who was misbehaving, and when he went to whack the horse it reared up and hit him on the head with its hoof. There was a lot of blood and Davey was very groggy, but he was determined to get to Deadmans Hut, so Alan helped him up onto a different horse. When the pair were crossing the Hollyford River, Alan remembers that blood from Davey's head was running down his horse's leg.[26]

Arriving at Deadmans, Alan had helped Davey off his horse and Davey said, 'Just light a fire, boy, and I'll be all right.' Then he asked him to get a sack and place it in front of the fire. Davey lay down on the sack.

Alan got back on his little black mare and hightailed it up the road to Marian Camp, 14 kilometres away – 'I would have won the Melbourne Cup that day.' He found the roadman at the camp and gasped out the story of Davey's accident. The man didn't respond but turned to an old winding telephone, which he rang. When it was answered he simply said, 'Davey Gunn's hurt. He's at Deadmans Hut,' and then hung up. Alan was somewhat floored by the man's lack of reaction and, not knowing if anything was going to happen or what else to do, he set off back to Deadmans. He was just about there when he heard a V8 truck bouncing down the road. It was a Public Works Department vehicle. Two men got out, crossed the footbridge to Deadmans, bandaged Davey's head, then walked him across the bridge back to the truck. On the way Davey stopped to talk to Alan. 'I'll be all right, I'll be back in a few days. Go round all the huts and stock them up with firewood.'

Alan was happy to oblige but first he had to deal with Willie, the horse that had kicked Davey and was still tied up at Hendersons Camp. When the horse had heard the V8 truck go past it had tried to bolt and had upset its load. Alan got back to find a dejected-looking horse covered with dripping treacle. He was frightened of the beast but eventually managed to undo the loads and bridle and let it go. Willie took off and wasn't seen for several months, but he did eventually come back.

Davey was in hospital for quite a while, after which he went to see his family in Oamaru. Meanwhile Alan kept himself busy stocking the huts with firewood, making sure he stacked it the way Davey did – sloping to help it dry out. In 1941, when Alan turned 18, he got his call-up letter and left for the barracks in Invercargill. When he entered the barracks he was greeted with: 'Here's the man who saved Davey Gunn's life.' 'How do you know that?' asked a bewildered Alan. 'Oh, everyone knows about it,' was the reply.[27]

Sometimes Davey would offer jobs to acquaintances or friends he met while he was 'out'. When he bumped into 66-year-old John Murtagh, who had worked for him before, he promptly offered him a job. Murtagh started work on 14 January 1943, and a couple of weeks later Davey, Murtagh and

Davey outside Deadmans Hut at about the time that he met Ruth Benstead.

Gordon Speden Collection

Ian Speden, Ruth Benstead and Davey at Deadmans, December 1943.

Gordon Speden Collection

a 'youth' named Bill Clements were packing stores into the Upper Pyke. During the afternoon of the third day (31 January) the three men were plodding along the river flats near Lake Wilmot when Murtagh suddenly lurched and fell off his horse. He had suffered a heart attack and, despite attempts by Davey and Clements to assist, he was dead within a couple of minutes. Davey knew he had to had to alert the authorities and get the body out to the road-end.[28]

He tied Murtagh's body onto a packhorse and began the 50-kilometre trek to Hendersons Camp. They got to Barrier Hut the first night, and the next day travelled on to Pyke Hut. At each overnight camp the body had to be lifted off the pack-horse and put back on again the next morning. Davey and Clements made good time and, after putting the body in a hut at Hendersons Camp, rode on to Marian Camp and reported the accident at 8.20 p.m. on 2 February. The policeman at Lumsden took the details and the following day the local coroner arrived at Hendersons Camp to record Davey's and Clements' state-ments. After a post-mortem the cause of death was registered as heart disease.[29]

When Davey's nephew Doug Gunn started working for him after the war he heard the story about Murtagh's death. Doug, who adopted Murtagh's dog Ben, was told that the weather at the time was very hot and that by the time they had got the body down to Lake Alabaster it had blown up and Davey had

A riding party on the way to Martins Bay in 1937. Ruth Benstead is third from right.
Murray Gunn Collection

had to make some cuts in the body to release gas from the abdomen.[30] There is no mention of this in the inquest report. Was it true or did Davey's friends embellish the story?

By now Davey was being described as 'well known', and was widely respected for his part in the rescue at Big Bay as well as for his outback lifestyle.[31] Stories such as this only added to his reputation and helped attract visitors to the area, further promoting Davey's overriding dream: to make the Hollyford a tourism destination.

Davey (left) with Ruth Benstead and Bill Denholm.
Murray Gunn Collection

Chapter Seven

Davey's Dream: Tourism

Only the finer type of person goes down the Hollyford.[1]

Davey loved the Hollyford and was confident that others would too. He was keen to share his wonderful area and, since his arrival in the district, had helped climbers and trampers by transporting stores, letting them use his huts and hiring them horses.

Most visitors to the area were, by necessity, hardy travellers. In the 1920s and early 1930s the usual route to Martins Bay was from Queenstown to Elfin Bay via a steamer, then up the Greenstone Valley, over the Greenstone Saddle and down Pass Creek track to the Hollyford River, a trip that took two or three days. From Deadmans Hut it was a three- to five-day trip down the valley to Martins Bay. Given the need to retrace their steps, trampers had to carry at least 10 days' food, and probably quite a bit more to allow for hold-ups owing to bad weather.

Such travellers must have been pleased to come across Davey or one of his workers – at the very least for directions and perhaps for a welcome meal if the party's food supplies were dwindling.

It seems that Davey and his former partner Patrick Fraser had always planned to tap into the tourism potential of the Hollyford. As early as October 1926 the Dunedin district manager of the Department of Tourist and Health Resorts was writing that the new owners of the 'Martins Bay Estate' had plans regarding tourism in the area.[2]

In September 1927 James Roberts, son of Sir John Roberts, Davey's neighbour and mortgagor at Sutton, was said to be

A riding party on the beach at Big Bay, 1937.

Murray Gunn Collection

forming a company with the idea of taking tourists through the Routeburn and Hollyford Tracks, but nothing seems to have come of this. Davey supported anything that brought people to the valley, whether it was tramping, mountaineering, scientific enquiry or mineral exploration. In 1930 he helped build a cage across the Hollyford River near Hidden Falls so that climbers had access to the Darran Mountains. Gordon Speden and his climbing companions were the first to use it when they made the second ascent of Mt Tutoko in December 1931.[3]

By early 1935 brothers Arthur and Wilfred Hamilton, who owned a sports store in Invercargill, were leasing huts in the upper Hollyford, near the Homer Tunnel area, where they had a guide stationed. Although it is not known who approached whom, the following year the Hamiltons were acting as agents for Davey, booking horses, huts and guides for trips down the Hollyford Valley to Martins Bay. In 1936 Davey took his first party – 12 visitors – down the Hollyford Valley to Martins Bay.[4]

To avoid the 'Demon Trail' along the side of Lake McKerrow, Davey purchased a launch, probably with assistance from the Hamilton brothers, which was taken around to Martins Bay on the government steamer.[5] This converted lifeboat with a cabin on it was called *Fiordland*, and a ride up or down the lake cost 7s 6d.[6] If the launch wasn't available, Davey would take small parties down the lake in one of his dinghies – not a trip for the faint-hearted if the weather was rough.

As the road inched its way towards Milford, access to the Hollyford Valley became easier. In the summer of 1937–38 Arthur and Wilfred Hamilton were advertising a 'new scenic route' to Martins Bay that involved only a three-hour walk from Marian Corner to Deadmans Hut, where the first night was spent. The second night could be spent at Hidden Falls or Pyke Hut, and the following day, after walking to the head of Lake McKerrow, visitors could take a launch ride down the lake to

Arthur Hamilton (right) at Hidden Falls Hut with white-baiter Tom Cameron, about 1938.

Arthur Bradshaw Collection

Building new sleeping
quarters at Martins Bay,
about 1941.
Murray Gunn Collection

Martins Bay. Trampers were encouraged to explore Martins Bay
for several days before retracing their route back up the valley.
The charge was 12s 6d per person per day, with a guide available
at £1 per day per party.

The huts that Davey had built in the Upper Pyke opened
up another opportunity – a round trip. By 1937 the Hamilton
brothers were also advertising a 10-day riding trip that followed
a circuit from Deadmans Hut to Martins Bay, then on to Big
Bay, through to the Upper Pyke and then down the river to the
Lower Pyke and back to Deadmans. Participants were met with
horses at Marian Camp on the Eglinton–Milford road, and the
cost was £10 for 10 days, including guide, food and horses.[7]

In order to accommodate the large groups that the Hamilton
brothers were bringing in, Davey enlarged the sleeping quarters
at Deadmans, Hidden Falls and Martins Bay Huts so that each
could accommodate 20 people.[8] While providing shelter and
some comfort, these huts were fairly basic. As Davey wrote in a
later brochure:

> Probably on no other New Zealand tourist route do the
> huts give the same backwoods impression that they do in
> the Hollyford. Built with rough bush material, [with] large
> chimneys for wood fires and cooking, they give a pioneer
> atmosphere which visitors enjoy.[9]

The floors were simply compacted earth, and the furniture was rough-hewn or made out of recycled timber boxes. The bunks consisted of saplings, timber slats or wire netting covered with dried fern fronds.[10] Blankets were supplied so that walkers only had to carry their personal gear, but over time these blankets became a little grubby and experienced visitors knew to bring something to cover the blankets near their faces.[11] The Hamiltons employed three guides during the summer, one of whom was the indefatigable Hugh McKenzie. Unguided walkers could buy meals for 3s 6d from the caretaker/guide at the huts.[12]

Most visitors were charmed by the experience. In January 1937 Davey guided a riding party of five on the circular trip down the Hollyford Valley to Martins Bay and back via the Pyke Valley. All were impressed by the scenery, the sure-footed horses, and the flounders for breakfast at Martins Bay: a 'delightful round trip'.[13]

Important early visitors were author Elsie K. Morton, who returned regularly, and Christchurch photographer Thelma Kent, who visited the area with a group of women friends in about 1936 and whose photographs provide a valuable record of Davey's huts.

The huts themselves were sometimes of enormous interest to the visitors. McKerrow Hut was an old surveyors' building

Loading the *Fiordland* at the head of Lake McKerrow, January 1944. By now the launch was starting to look a little the worse for wear.
Gordon Speden Collection

Elsie K. Morton with Davey at Deadmans, about 1937.
Murray Gunn Collection

that had been shifted up the lake from Jamestown.[14] A group that arrived there in January 1938 described it as 'a marvellous place . . . Everything seemed to date back something B.C. The hut was full of antiques. We had quite an interesting time looking round and discussing what certain objects may be and what they may be used for.'[15]

People's accounts of their trips spurred others to visit and the trips became well patronised, particularly during school and university holidays.

Despite the provision of guides, huts and packhorses, the trip was still something of an adventure. 'I.S.' recounted a riding trip in February 1938, when in one day the guide took the group from Upper Pyke Hut to Big Bay and then on to Martins Bay, where they finally arrived at 3 a.m. On their way back to Deadmans the same party had two packhorses disappear down a side track in the hope of avoiding the climb over the Little Homer Saddle. When the trampers tried to head them off, the horses plunged into the Hollyford River and swam to the other side. They were recovered the next day, minus one saddle and both packs. The visitors had only the clothes they were standing up in for their trip back to Dunedin. The packs were later found and returned to their owners.[16]

One of Davey's dinghies near Jamestown in much calmer weather than Arnold Grey experienced on his trip down the lake.

Murray Gunn Collection

Arnold Grey, who went on a fishing trip with his father in the late 1930s, described the journey down Lake McKerrow in a dinghy as 'one of the most harrowing trips of my life'. They had a makeshift sail hoisted and were running before a strong easterly. Davey's worker in charge of the boat had a penknife ready in case he needed to cut the flax cord holding the sail. The boat roared down the lake, which was so rough that one of the dogs in the front was seasick. When the boat was about 150 metres from the shore the dogs could not wait a moment later. They leapt out and swam to shore.[17]

World War Two put paid to the growth in the Hollyford tourism trade. Cars had become a popular way for New Zealanders to see the country, but petrol rationing meant that travelling to Te Anau became nearly impossible. The Milford Track and the hostel at Milford Sound were closed for the entire period of the war.[18] In any case, Davey would have had trouble finding guides and caretakers – he could barely find enough musterers, who were essential to his livelihood. So Davey spent the war years concentrating on his cattle and the huts; the tracks received little attention.

He was still thinking about tourists, though. During the summer of 1941–42 Davey and Derek Turnbull spent time clearing a track from Deadmans to the Harris Saddle. This would give walkers who arrived via the Greenstone Valley an alternative means of getting back to Lake Wakatipu and the steamer. Davey also had dreams of cutting a track through to Milford Sound and went on a reconnaissance trip with Turnbull in the early 1940s. It would be another 10 years before Davey added this route to his brochure.[19]

After the war, holidays became popular again and Davey had plenty of workers; the Hollyford seemed to attract returned servicemen who had difficulty settling. The partnership with the Hamilton brothers of Invercargill was not resurrected, but relations between them and Davey remained friendly. Instead, Davey teamed up with Gerry Hamilton (no relation), an Englishman who, in his own words, was 'disinclined for a conventional existence' after the war.[20]

Gerry Hamilton, about 1945.
Doug Gunn

Gerry was a well-built, well-spoken, ginger-haired man with a good sense of humour and a pleasant manner. He was also described as quiet, intelligent, and an alcoholic.[21] The arrangement seems to have been that Gerry was in charge of the tourism side of the business and that he and Davey would split the profits made from the guided trips. This allowed Davey to focus on cattle. He hated writing letters, but Gerry Hamilton was happy to do so. He kept a typewriter at Deadmans Hut and produced promotional material, including an article for the *Wide World Magazine* (London), glamorising Davey's life in the Hollyford.[22]

In September 1945 Gerry wrote to schools, hospitals and other potential customers to advise them that Davey was re-opening the Hollyford Valley to tourists. Bookings could be made directly with Gunn and himself, or through the government Tourist Department in Invercargill. The fact that the facilities were a little run down and the track was not marked was given a positive spin in the letter, which stated that 'a measure of uncertainty should add to your enjoyment':[23]

> The scenery of the Valley is well known, and, by the unanimous opinion of those who have visited it, the finest in New Zealand. We hope that you will become one of their number.[24]

The time was right and in late 1945 three large parties made the trip, along with several smaller groups, making a total of 80–100 visitors. Every year the number increased and in the summer of 1949–50 more than 300 walkers made the journey. Tourists were now coming from much further afield than Otago and Southland. New Zealand visitors were coming from as far away as Kaitaia, and the 1951 season included visitors from Britain and Malaya.[25]

However, visitors' expectations were increasing and they were sometimes disappointed at what they were getting for their money. Doug Gunn remembered that when walkers got to Hidden Falls they would say things like, 'Imagine paying a pound a day for this.' But although the first night was often a shock, most people got on and enjoyed it, as Elisabeth Tongue recorded in her diary. At Hidden Falls she said, 'These bunks are made of wood slats and were built for Davy's musterers. Feel a

A group of South Otago High School pupils and guide Ross Speden pose on plane wreckage at Big Bay, 1950.

Peter Robson

Guide Derek Turnbull (centre front) with the Wanderers Tramping Club, Christmas 1947.

Derek and Pat Turnbull Collection

bit tired and low, huts dirty . . . but situation of course improves next morning.'[26]

Ed Cotter was one guide who felt nervous about visitors' reactions:

> I took a few tours through for him and they were mainly young people. I was terribly distressed at having to take them into the huts. When they arrived and found that it was just fern bunks it was quite difficult for them to appreciate that they were in the wilds so suddenly.[27]

Davey obviously expected others to be as tough as he was. On hearing that some trampers were complaining about the draughty sleeping quarters at McKerrow Hut (which at this stage had canvas walls and was subject to the strong winds that blow up Lake McKerrow), Davey was dismissive: 'Some of them don't mind roughing it a bit, but some of them will complain about anything.'[28]

Davey's habit of forgoing lunch was not to everyone's taste, as 'Popeye' Lucas observed: 'Dav[e]y Gunn was as tough as old boots, and expected no less from his tramping parties . . . he believed in a big feed in the morning and another one at night: Stopping at midday to boil the billy was for sissies.'[29]

His frugality with food also took some of the shine off

The Speden family at McKerrow Hut in 1947. Note the canvas walls on the sleeping quarters.

Gordon Speden Collection

for some people, who did not appreciate having to pick mouse droppings out of their porridge.[30] Cotter remembered one hungry group:

> We got a crowd down from St Andrew's College and they arrived at Hidden Falls Hut, where I was working, for lunch. I remember the kids asking me for more to eat. Probably all they had was porridge or bread for breakfast before they started for Pyke. Davey Gunn's favourite saying to anyone who was hungry was, 'We should eat to live, not live to eat.' It didn't go down very well with a load of fourth-formers.[31]

Nonetheless, the parties were usually well supplied with venison stews, pea-meal soups and tinned fruit. When they were near the coast there might also be seafood. In her account of a 10-day trip in February 1955 Patience Lang noted what they ate for evening meals:

1st day   cold meat and potatoes, peaches and milk
2nd day   stew, prunes and custard
3rd day   pea soup and corn beef, prunes and custard
4th day   cold meat, peas and potatoes, sultana milk pudding
5th day   tinned fish and potatoes, apple slices and prunes
6th day   stew, sago made with treacle
7th day   tinned fish, apple pie
8th day   stew, apricots and custard
9th day   soup, cold meat and potatoes, apple slices and milk[32]

A bit basic, but pretty good food for a tramping holiday.

Martins Bay was usually everyone's favourite place. The scenery was grand, the weather usually mild, and people could fish, go floundering, spear eels or explore the old McKenzie homestead. And, because it had been supplied by coastal steamer, it was the best-equipped hut. The living room was comfortable and the bunkroom had mattresses. There was a second bunkroom with a fireplace, and a large shed for storing saddles and drying clothes. The main hut had a kitchen stocked with rolls of bacon, tins of meat, fish, butter, milk and jam. There were also packets of jelly, cornflour, Weet-Bix, custard powder and bottles of sauce.[33]

In early 1947 Gerry Hamilton was fired, after drinking the contents of a parcel of sherry, rum and gin bottles that he was carrying in for a tramping club.[34] Davey then asked his nephew Doug, who had been working as a musterer and guide, to become his partner in the tourism business. Doug would take over organising the trips and the guides, arranging the buses, replying to letters and keeping a record of all bookings.[35]

The guides at this time were paid £1 a day plus keep, which Doug said was quite good money. The average wage at the time was about £5 per week. Many of Davey's guides were family friends, often from Gore, or students looking for holiday employment. Ian Speden was both, and agreed that Davey paid quite well. It wasn't as good as the freezing works, but you saved more, and 'It was an interesting job, handling horses, doing the cooking and you met lots of people.'[36]

Doug Gunn, Davey's nephew, who in 1947 replaced the disgraced Gerry Hamilton as Davey's partner in the tourism operation.

Doug Gunn

The old chair across the Pyke River before the mechanism broke in 1945, after about 60 years' service.

Murray Gunn Collection

For Davey and his men it was a never-ending job keeping the tracks clear. Said Olga Sansom, 'Davey never walked the track without blasting away some rock or other from a bluff, or fixing a log-bridge . . . It was his great ambition to have good huts and all-weather tracks right through the valley.'[37] During trips the guides would clear trees out of the way for their parties, but winter was the time when most of the track work was done.

The 'Demon Trail', in particular, suffered 'continual slips, washouts and a tangle of fallen timber'.[38] After it had been neglected during the war, Gerry Hamilton told the Department of Tourist and Health Resorts that it would take a couple of men two months to get the track back to its pre-war state.[39] In October 1946 Davey applied to the department for a grant of £50 to repair the 'Demon Trail'. While the department looked favourably on the application, it was not granted because work on the Routeburn Track was thought to be more urgent.[40]

In 1945 the wire rope and chair across the Pyke River, built in about 1884, collapsed because one of the wire ropes had rusted through. The Pyke is a dangerous river to cross, and without a bridge there would sooner or later be loss of life. Davey appealed to the Lake County Council for assistance with replacing the chair, and received a paltry £25. With this amount of money it was impossible to replace the chair, so Davey had to think about how he could repair it. He had two men working for him at the time, and he asked Gordon Speden to come in and help as well.[41]

In August 1945 the four men set to work constructing a bridge. One of the cables from the collapsed chair was re-used and another 250-foot-long cable was made by twisting together four or five strands of No. 8 fencing wire. Speden remembered that this was painful work.[42] The cables were strung across the river and tightened. The men then made decking by splitting timber from the surrounding bush. Gordon, who was a timber merchant, suggested spacing the planks out, or else the bridge would have two or three tons of timber on it, but Davey assured him it would be all right. By the time the bridge was finished it had cost Davey £100 (on top of the council grant) in wages and materials.[43]

Sadly, the bridge did not last long. It had a large sag and no wind bracing, and the weight of the decking imposed a severe load on the light cables. Within two months the structure was in ruins after strong winds broke one of the fencing-wire cables and the planking thrashed itself loose.[44] It was back to square one.

It was about this time that Davey enlisted the help of the Member of Parliament for Gore, Thomas Lachlan Macdonald, who was a friend of Gordon Speden's and was to become a

Davey's replacement bridge across the Pyke, which survived for only two months.

good friend to Davey. On 13 August 1947 Macdonald wrote to Mr Parry, the Minister of Internal Affairs, seeking assistance for Davey. He followed this up with a second letter five days later, enclosing additional information and Davey's estimates of the amounts required to fix the track and repair the Pyke bridge. He ended the letter by informing the minister that over 200 people had been down the Hollyford in the past year and that the area was becoming 'more and more popular with trampers'.[45]

Macdonald's letters had the desired effect and a Public Works Department engineer was instructed to investigate. He reported that the cost of erecting a suspension footbridge was prohibitive (£1,200), but that installing another cable and chair system would cost only £150 in materials. He further estimated that repairing the track from Deadmans to Martins Bay would cost about £377. A follow-up letter from Macdonald to the minister saw two grants announced in March: £150 to replace the Pyke chair and £350 to clear the track from Deadmans Hut to Martins Bay.[46]

In connection with the proposal to rebuild the Pyke chair the Public Works Department suggested that a new boat be purchased for transporting materials on Lake McKerrow. The launch that Davey used was, they said, in poor condition and 'quite unsuitable for carrying any heavy material'. At least a third of the boat's ribs were missing and it leaked badly.[47] The tireless Thomas Macdonald had already persuaded the Minister for Marine to reinstate the pre-war six-monthly supply-boat visits to Martins Bay, and it was proposed to deliver the boat to Martins Bay this way.

Unfortunately, however, the skipper of the government ship *Matai* had no experienced hand for boat work and didn't like the look of the weather, so the cable and new dinghy were left at Bluff when the *Matai* departed on its run. The 14-foot dinghy was eventually delivered to the Hollyford Valley by road, which meant taking it down the Hollyford River – a feat never before attempted. Twelve of Davey's friends from Invercargill came to help with the task.[48]

One mile into its river trip the boat had to be manpowered past some rapids. It was pushed across timber skids and at some places carried on poles cut from the bush. Below the rapids the boat was put into the river and Davey and some of the men took it down to the flats near Humboldt Creek. The next day they sailed down the river as far as the rapids between Hidden Falls and the Pyke River. To get around these dangerous rapids the boat was carried for about 400 metres through the bush. From there it was taken downriver to Lake McKerrow, a journey of 30 kilometres overall.

It was a new experience for Davey, who had never been

MP Tom Macdonald on a visit to the Hollyford during the 1940s.

Gordon Speden Collection

Peter Robson and Donald West on the new Pyke chair, 1953.

Peter Robson

down the section of river from Hidden Falls to Little Homer Falls. There was some danger involved, as the current was swift in places and there were innumerable snags where trees had fallen into the river. At one point the boat was caught on a snag and only freed after much levering and pulling. The resulting hole was patched by Walter Wallis, who had thoughtfully brought along some sheet copper for just such an emergency. The safe arrival of the boat at the lake was suitably celebrated and Davey enjoyed the whole experience.[49]

The boat was named *Gratitude*, for reasons explained in the following excerpt from Ron Stewart's summary of the event:

> The boat it lay at Sunny Creek
> But needed at McKerrow
> They couldn't float it down the stream
> Or put it on a barrow.
>
> The mode of transport it was slow,
> We had to pull and push
> The war-cry was 'Heave-ho!'
> Through rocky bluffs and bush.
>
> Arthur was our leader,
> There is no need to say

His knowledge of the Outdoor,
(And this is by the way)
Extends from Stewart Island
Right up to Jacksons Bay.

We can't forget our Davey
The King of all the land,
With a grin from here to breakfast time,
And an axe stuck in his hand.

There was a guy called Bigwood
Whose remarks were by the way,
'It's physical impossibility
To take it all that way.'

So remember all you trampers
Who rowing to Martins Bay
And think of us with 'Gratitude'
Of how we slaved that day.[50]

The ability to cater for tourists and make an income from them was becoming increasingly important to Davey. The impact of deer, which had first appeared in the valley in about 1935, was becoming severe by the late 1940s.[51] During the war very few had been shot and deer numbers increased rapidly.

Davey (left) with Harry Turnbull, Gerry Hamilton, Val Bigwood and Ron Stewart at Hidden Falls.

Derek and Pat Turnbull Collection

The deer competed with the cattle for food, and by 1949 the poulation was so high that Davey was forced to reduce cattle numbers so they wouldn't starve. Over an estimated 1,200 acres he had only about 400 cattle, about 200 of them breeding cows. The cows were spread through the various blocks, with about 40 near the hut at Martins Bay and a similar number at each of the Kaipo, McKenzies, Big Bay and the Upper Pyke.[52] Having them so scattered involved a lot of work and travel, but no single area could support them all.

Fewer breeding cows, of course, meant fewer young beasts to take out to the sales, and Davey's income must have been affected. Not that he would ever have discussed this with anybody. When Doug Gunn left the tourism partnership in the late 1940s his uncle owed him £100. Some months later, when Doug saw Davey in Oamaru, Davey gave him £50 and Doug realised that this was all he was going to get.[53] Davey wouldn't have been able to tell Doug straight that this was all he could afford.

Chapter Eight

The Busy Years

Your attention is drawn to the fact that the licence is purely a temporary one and can be cancelled at any time.[1]

In 1950 Davey was 62 and still tough and strong, with hardly any grey hair. One of the only signs of ageing was that he'd had to give up shooting. He had been a crack shot but, because he was becoming long-sighted, he could no longer use the open sights on his Martini Henry .303 rifle. He also began to feel the cold and was eventually persuaded to use a sleeping bag instead of the horse-cover or blanket he had always made do with.[2]

Twenty-five years on, Davey's leases were still haunting him. Runs 471–474, which included much of the Hollyford Valley and the area around Lake Alabaster, had been leased for 21 years from 1 March 1929. They were about to run out and the government was keener than ever to add the area to a proposed national park. The leases were renewed in December 1949 but only for two and a half years, which signalled clearly that the Department of Lands and Survey did not regard the runs as a long-term farming prospect. Davey's grazing licences from the Forest Service for the Upper Pyke and Big Bay areas were still on a year-to-year basis, and his temporary grazing licence for 2,000 acres in the Deadmans/Hidden Falls area was due to expire on 30 June 1952.[3] The uncertainty of his farming operation must have weighed heavily on Davey, but he discussed it with no one close, so none of his friends or family was aware of how precarious things were.

One evening in September 1950 Davey was out on the steep slopes above Deadmans Hut, trying to encourage a steer down to the flats, when he lost his footing and fell over a bluff, landing on a narrow ledge. Initial reports gave his fall as being a rather unbelievable 60–90 metres, but later accounts talked about nine metres. Being a horseman, he instinctively tried to fall loosely, and perhaps this saved his life. But Davey was dazed and winded, and when he tried to move he found he 'could do so only with the greatest difficulty and pain'.[4]

Luckily, Jim Speden was down at Deadmans Hut. He was not alarmed by Davey's failure to return by nightfall but became worried when his boss hadn't arrived back by dawn. At first light Jim went out to search for him. He followed Davey's horse tracks and found the horse still tethered where it had been left the previous morning. Jim climbed the hill and, as he got higher, was greeted by Davey's dogs. He called out but, as Davey could only make croaking noises, it took some time for Jim to locate him. He then had to get Davey down the steep slope and back to Deadmans Hut. Broken ribs and a damaged spine made the descent painful enough, but the kilometre-long ride on horseback to the hut was excruciating – even Davey described it as 'very painful'.[5]

Speden made Davey as comfortable as possible and set out to Marian Camp to use the phone. By late afternoon a rescue party had arrived, including Dr L. G. Bell of Lumsden. The doctor did what he could for Davey and then, as the bridges had been washed away in a recent flood, Davey was stretchered out 7 kilometres to Access Creek, where an ambulance from Invercargill was waiting.

The stretcher trip was gruelling for the patient and for the men carrying him, first getting the stretcher across the swing-bridge in front of the hut and then along several bouldery stream-beds up the valley to the ambulance. As soon as the party reached the ambulance Davey was given morphine for the long ambulance ride. He reached Southland Hospital at 3 a.m., 33 hours after his accident.[6]

X-rays showed that he had several fractured ribs, damage to one lung, multiple bruising and a spinal injury 'near enough to being a broken neck'. When Ray Wilson visited Davey in hospital he saw Davey's chest and said it looked as if it had been painted black: 'there was not a piece of white skin anywhere'.[7]

Davey was a month in hospital, where he was the centre of much attention, even warranting a media report:

Musterers Jim Sinclair (left)
and Jim Speden, 1949.
Eric Midgley

RESCUER NOW AMONG THE RESCUED

Mr David Gunn, the 63-year-old hero of many recorded and unrecorded rescues of trampers and others isolated or injured in the treacherous country of the Lower Hollyford Valley, is today among the rescued.[8]

He got special treatment from the hospital staff and received plenty of visitors. One of the first to visit was Graham Frederic, who had been injured in the Hollyford the previous Easter and was 'among the long list' of people rescued by Davey. On a Sunday Davey would have up to 30 visitors, and Jim Speden commented that 'it was like going to a levee, visiting Davey, I felt that his many friends should move past his bed in a procession each one bowing to him'. Even people who hadn't met Davey wrote and wished him well. Jim Sinclair went into the Hollyford to do the spring muster, as Davey he was going to be out of action for some time.[9]

A poem appeared in one of the local newspapers:

BLUFF FALL

A welcome now to Davey Gunn
In hospital reposing,
Instead of tramping through the bush
He's lying down and dozing
I'm also told at least one eye
Is black and slowly closing.

For Davey he fell down a bluff
And suffered some abrasions
His tactics as he nose-dived down
Embodied no evasions
He took the packet, but it was
Just one of his occasions.

Davey Gunn lives way out west
A man of some renown
He sometimes drives a mob of steers
Two-hundred miles to town
He may fall somewhat heavy, but
You cannot hold him down.[10]

Davey's wife, Ethel, and son Murray travelled from Oamaru
to visit him, but when he left hospital Davey chose to convalesce

Davey with Alice and Harry
Turnbull, about 1949.
Derek and Pat Turnbull Collection

Davey with Bess, one of his favourite dogs, 1951.

Derek and Pat Turnbull Collection

with his friends Alice and Harry Turnbull, near Invercargill.[11] He was advised not to return to the Hollyford too soon and stayed with the Turnbulls for six weeks, but Davey felt that he would only recover completely back in his beloved Hollyford. He'd been away 10 weeks – the longest he had been 'out' in nearly 25 years, and it was time to go home.[12]

The fall and resulting injuries took their toll. Before the accident Davey was said to look 15 years younger than he was, but after it he began to feel his age. Rather than running up and down hills, he now walked quickly. The spinal injury had left his head bowed, but corrective exercises put that right within a couple of years.[13]

Davey had only been back in the Hollyford for a couple of months when his mother, Isabella, died at Waimate, on 9 February 1951, aged 91. Davey did not attend the funeral but was in Waimate by 22 February, when he signed affidavits for the probate of his mother's will. Isabella had instructed that her assets (£700) were to be divided equally between her five children.[14] That alone would have been welcomed by Davey, but more important was the fact that his father's estate, which had been left in trust to Isabella during her lifetime, could now be settled. The relevant papers have not survived, but it is likely that Alexander's estate (valued at £8,000 in 1932) would have yielded some money for Davey.[15] This income may have been the impetus for his attempts to improve the services for tourists, and the next few years were to be busy ones.

One of things Davey did was to sort out a more suitable base for his tourism operations. Deadmans Hut was not big enough to cope with the increasing numbers of tourists and, if the river was in flood, it was difficult getting the laden packhorses across. The solution was to take over Hendersons Camp, which was just a short distance up the road.

In 1951 Davey arranged to purchase the camp from the Public Works Department. Only 15 of the original 25 cabins were still standing, and Davey paid £180 – £12 for each. Many of the fittings, such as stoves, windows and tubs, had been removed by departing holiday-makers presumably desperate for house parts during postwar shortages. Davey equiped the cabins in his usual style: Cyclone netting on the beds with straw-filled mattresses, and wooden boxes for seats. The camp had pit toilets, three tin basins for washing and a copper to supply hot water. He renamed it Hollyford Camp.[16]

There was no communal dining hut so Davey employed his two nephews, Doug and Clarence, to build one. Once again, materials were recycled and 'found'. Iron and flooring were salvaged from another abandoned PWD camp, and the piles and beams were made from local broadleaf and red beech trees. Davey gave Doug and Clarence several tins of bent and rusty nails (which he had probably been saving for years), but as soon as he left, Clarence bravely ordered some new nails to be sent in. The PWD offered Davey a big range for the communal hut, but Davey told them 'we don't want it, people come in here to rough it' so the hut had a simple open fire.[17]

A visitor to the new base recorded her impressions:

> [We] reached Hendersons Camp where Dav[e]y occupied
> some roadmakers' huts for his headquarters. The main hut

Davey and Ed Cotter leaving Davey's new camp at the start of a muster. The new communal hut is in the background on the left.
Ed Cotter

is still being completed. Dave, Jean, Jack and Ian Speden welcome us. Lots of pack-horses graze outside. A big wood fire heats the kettle for a welcome tea. We settle into small two-man huts after pushing out sheltering horses! Dinner is venison (wild) stew, the first of many such meals.[18]

Davey had not had the huts at Hendersons Camp long when there was a period of very heavy rain. Gordon Speden remembers being woken at four in the morning by Davey saying, 'The huts are gone!' 'What huts? You can't catch me with that one, you're just making an excuse to get me out of bed,' Speden replied. 'No. Come on, get up!' Sure enough, the river was running in among the huts, and three or so had floated away off their rotten piles.[19]

In November or December of 1951 a woman arrived who was to become important in Davey's life. Jean Prust was from Melbourne, and had worked as a nurse in Europe during World War Two. She was slim but tough, with blue eyes and 'a very determined Aussie jaw'. Jean was 40 when she came to New Zealand in about 1950, intending to spend a year exploring each island. She arrived in the Hollyford on a 10-day walking tour and said that as soon as she arrived 'it felt so right'. Even before the tour started Jean had decided 10 days would not be

Jean Prust trekking to the Kaipo River.
Ed Cotter

enough and asked Davey if she could stay on. He invited her along on the next muster.[20]

After the 10-day tour Jean must have gone out to get the luggage she had stored somewhere, because Doug Gunn remembers her arriving with two big suitcases. The men asked what she was doing and Davey told them that she was going to look after the hut at Martins Bay, but that did not happen. After the muster Jean stayed at Deadmans and at Hollyford Camp, where she cooked for tourists and organised the food provisions for each hut. She was very efficient and in time helped run the tourism operation.[21]

It was the 1950s and people were mostly very discreet about extra-marital affairs. Davey and Jean were no exception. Both were intensely private people and their relationship was never openly discussed. Only those who spent a lot of time in the Hollyford guessed what was going on. Ed Cotter, who saw Davey give Jean a kiss before heading down the valley for a few days, witnessed a rare public show of affection.[22]

Murray met Jean when he visited the Hollyford. The pair didn't get on, but Murray admitted: 'She gave my father comforts he had never had before, like washing his clothes and cooking his meals and so on.'[23] When Ethel heard that Jean was living in the Hollyford she was understandably upset, according to Murray:

> My mother knew that Jean was living in the Hollyford. She wasn't pleased about it but I said this sort of situation is inevitable with him living over there and you living here so she had to leave it at that, but Jean drove a wedge between my father and me.[24]

Ethel was not the only woman to be upset by Jean's residence. Ruth Benstead had been coming to the Hollyford for her summer holiday for 14 years, and when she arrived in early January 1952 Jean had been there for a month or so. This must have been unsettling for Ruth, but she was her usual friendly self. The plan was for a group, including Davey, Jean and Ruth, to head down to Martins Bay and travel back to Deadmans via Big Bay. Jack Jenkins was travelling ahead of the group and had great delight in telling Davey's workers and friends that Davey was coming around 'with his two girlfriends'.[25] Before the group left Ruth had commented to Doug Gunn: 'I hear that

Davey with (from left) Alice
Turnbull, Ruth Benstead and
Jean Prust before they set off
down the valley to Martins
Bay, January 1952.

Derek and Pat Turnbull Collection

you guys don't like Jean very much but she is treating me like a queen.' When Ruth got back to Deadmans it was a different story: 'Get rid of that bitch!' she said to Doug.[26]

All had been well until the group reached Martins Bay, where Jean and Ruth fell out. It is quite likely that Davey had not foreseen a problem, having failed to realise that Jean wanted to supplant Ruth in his affections. He probably underestimated the strength of one or both women's feelings for him, and he certainly would have found it difficult to talk to Ruth about it. Doug Gunn thought Davey was too much of a gentleman to intervene, but the situation was hard on Ruth, who left immediately and didn't return until after Davey's death. Doug saw her later in Christchurch and described her as 'heart-broken'.[27]

Some time after Jean's arrival in the Hollyford Davey's visits to Ethel in Oamaru ceased altogether. He was still aware of his responsibilities, and on what was probably his final visit in July 1953 he organised his will. Ethel was to continue to receive £250 a year for her lifetime, and the remainder of the estate to be divided between his three children on her death.[28]

On 4 January 1952 a party of 13 were heading from Martins Bay to McKerrow Hut with their guide Charlie Beagle, a quiet, thick-set man.[29] Eight of the party took a dinghy to Eight Mile Creek and walked on from there, while the remaining five elected to walk all the way from Martins Bay. After the walkers left, Beagle saddled up the packhorses, loaded them and followed on behind. The boat party saw them on the shore near Hokuri Creek and waved. Not far from this point two of the walkers, Lenore Algie and Daphne Williams, both aged 20 and from Oamaru, fell behind the other three. The track was well defined and the pair had made it clear they were quite happy to walk together, so the other three carried on to McKerrow Hut.

Beagle, who was coming up behind, met the boatman, Gillies, at Eight Mile Creek where the eight trampers had been dropped off. Gillies told him that all five trampers were ahead of him, so Beagle continued on his way. Soon after (at about 2.45 p.m.) he passed guide Jack Jenkins and his party, who were coming down the lake. Forty-five minutes later, Jenkins heard someone calling out in the bush. He investigated and found Algie and Williams about 10 metres below the track. He brought them back to the track and invited them to accompany his party to Martins Bay, but they wanted to carry on. Jenkins gave them directions and they set off. At this point they were about thee kilometres from Six Mile Creek and they had plenty of time to reach McKerrow Hut before dark. They had barley sugars and chocolate and carried sleeping bags.[30]

When Beagle reached McKerrow Hut at 7 p.m. he found that Algie and Williams had not arrived. When they still hadn't turned up by nightfall he decided they must have met Jenkins and decided to return to Martins Bay with his party.

During the night there was torrential rain and in the morning, when he went out to look for them, Beagle found the creeks too swollen to cross and was forced to return to the hut. The depleted party reached Hollyford Camp on 6 January and Beagle attempted to find out whether Algie and Williams were indeed with Jenkins's party. Someone rang Southern Scenic Air Services' Queenstown office and asked them to radio Martins Bay to check.

The alarm was raised and on 7 January the search began. Searchers included Charlie Beagle, Gillies, Fairbanks, Jenkins and others, including Frank Walsh from Dipton, who had just arrived in the valley to do some tramping. Two house surgeons from Dunedin Hospital, Robert Fraser and Thomas O'Donnell, flew into Martins Bay, along with Sergeant Matheson of the Queenstown police.

The story reached the media in the capital, Wellington:

GIRL TRAMPERS MISSING IN RUGGED FIORDLAND

An emergency rescue bid swung into action this morning. Ground search parties are moving over precipitous cliffs and across dangerous, high flowing streams on the mountain-side above the lake. Most of the searchers are professional guides assisted by trampers and radio-equipped planes from Southern Scenic Airtrips [*sic*], Queenstown.[31]

Jim Speden and Frank Walsh spent some time searching around Six Mile Creek, also known as Tomahawk Creek, 'a cataract which leapt and raced downhill at a great pace'. Just below where the track crossed the creek 'the water took a tremendous leap down'.[32] At 2.45 p.m. on 9 January the pair found Lenore Algie's body in Six Mile Creek, about 60 metres below the track.

Daphne Williams's pack was found a short distance downstream, but there was no sign of her. Bad weather hampered the search, which continued for several days. A rock pool close to where Six Mile Creek flows into Lake McKerrow was blasted to make an opening to allow the pool to drain, but without result.[33] Eventually the search was called off. Daphne Williams's body was found four months later at the head of Lake McKerrow, by Davey and Jack Jenkins.[34]

---

8   THE DOMINION, THURSDAY, JANUARY 10, 1952.

Searchers Find Body Of One Missing Girl Tramper In Lower Hollyford Creek

Pack Believed To Belong To Her Companion Picked Up Downstream

---

At the inquest on 22 July 1952 the cause of death of both women was given as drowning. It appears that they made slow progress on the 'Demon Trail'. Somehow Charlie Beagle had passed them. Perhaps they had lost the track by then, or perhaps they avoided the guide so they could walk at their own pace. For whatever reason, they had not reached the hut when the heavy rain started. According to one newspaper article five inches (110 millimetres) of rain fell while Algie and Williams were trying to get to the hut.[35] Given that the creeks were not swollen until after dark, and that Six Mile Creek is not very far from where Jack Jenkins saw the pair at 3.30 p.m., it seems likely that the women had decided to turn back at some point. They had then been hampered by darkness and drowned when they attempted to cross the swollen creek.

The coroner found no fault on the part of the guides, and rejected Lenore Algie's family's call for stricter regulations to control tramping. Having heard that the Algie family was intending to pursue this line, Murray Gunn arranged for legal representation for Davey at the inquest (which Davey did not attend). Davey presumably thought this was unnecessary, as he never thanked Murray for it.[36] Davey was, however, deeply affected by the deaths of the two women.

Despite this serious setback, Davey was still keen to further develop the area for tourists and he had an idea. In 1949 'Popeye' (Fred) Lucas of Southern Scenic Air Services had established an airstrip at Martins Bay with the idea of flying out the large quantities of whitebait that could be caught in the lower reaches of the Hollyford River. The airstrip was on land

'Popeye' Lucas (left) and Cecil Mitchell on the strip at Martins Bay. Lucas first landed on this strip on 26 August 1949.

Eric Midgley

A trip to see the old McKenzie homestead at Martins Bay was a popular excursion for visitors.

Ed Cotter

owned by the Catholic Church. Southern Scenic Air Services had not sought permission from the church to build the airstrip but presumably had discussed it with Davey, who had been paying rates on the land since 1931.[37]

Lucas had arranged for three brothers – Eric, Bert and Cecil Mitchell of Ross – to clear the land. It took the three experienced bushmen 10 days to clear the bush and rushes and to drain the boggy areas. On 26 August 1949 Lucas made his first landing at Martins Bay. The first airstrip proved too boggy and in 1950 Lucas, Tom Robertson and Bill Dennison built a more satisfactory one further north.

It appears that in early 1953 Southern Scenic Air Services, fearing competition from other whitebaiters and aircraft operators, tried to secure exclusive use of the airstrip.[38] Davey objected. He was interested in the idea of flying people into the district and could see potential in being able to transport tourists directly to Martins Bay, his most popular hut. Here they could fish, hunt, visit seal and penguin colonies, and see what was left of the old McKenzie homestead, which had been popularised in Alice MacKenzie's 1947 book about her childhood at Martins Bay.[39] When he could not reach an agreement with Lucas, Davey decided to build an airstrip of his own. His son, Murray, believed the airstrip was an act of desperation – an attempt to solve the issue of access if and when he lost his leases.[40]

Brian Swete (left) with Jack Jenkins and Eric Midgley at their hut at Big Bay.

Daphne Midgley

Once again Davey sought partners, probably lacking the necessary capital himself, and settled on Bill Hewett and Brian Swete. Both could see the tourism potential of an airstrip. They had been involved in the whitebait industry with 'Popeye' Lucas, and also saw an opportunity to fly whitebait out of Martins Bay in competition with Lucas.[41]

Hewett and Swete marked out a 1,000-metre strip 50 metres wide. Swete then spent three months working on his own clearing bush and blasting stumps. The partners purchased a McCormick Deering T20 crawler tractor, which had a hydraulic blade, for the next stage. The tractor was stripped down to one-ton loads and flown in to Martins Bay (onto Lucas's strip) in Hewett's Miles Aerovan. The tractor was re-assembled and Charlie Curran from Mossburn was flown in to operate it.[42]

Meanwhile, Davey somewhat belatedly went to Dunedin to arrange a lease with the Catholic Church. The church had been left the land by Father John Francis O'Donnell, of Queenstown, who had bought the property in the early 1900s with the intention of establishing a sawmill.[43] Although Davey had been paying rates on this land for at least 20 years, it seems church administrators may not have been aware that he was in occupation.

While in Dunedin Davey was interviewed by the *Evening Star* and took the opportunity to promote the huts, the nearly finished airstrip and the hunting and fishing in the area.[44]

By now the airstrip had cost the partners well over £1,000, and it was lack of funds that caused the project to founder.[45] Davey was probably at the limit of what he could contribute, but he was not about to tell his partners. Instead he insisted that primitive (i.e. cheap) facilities were what people wanted.

Ed Cotter recalled:

> They were discussing the kind of furniture they were going to have in the lodge they were going to build. Bill is telling Davey about the easy chairs that they are going to have for the tourists and Davey says, 'Well, I've always used apple

A letter from Davey to his friend Gordon Speden.

Gordon Speden Collection

The McCormick Deering crawler tractor rusting away near the Hollyford Tourist Company Lodge, 1961.

Mike Bennett

boxes and that's what we are going to have – apple boxes. That's what [the tourists] have wanted up till now and I don't see any reason to change.[46]

The project fell apart completely when Hewett and Swete discovered that Davey had made the lease in his name only. Hewett followed other ventures, but Swete, with no money left, had little option but to work for Davey mustering, track clearing, packing stores and guiding. He left in 1954 when he got a job packing stores on the Milford Track.[47]

The tractor remained, as it would have been expensive to fly it back out. Perhaps Davey bought his partners' shares, or perhaps he couldn't afford to. Either way, Murray recalled, the vehicle was left to rust: 'My father, not being mechanically minded, wasn't able to look after it. It broke down and just lay out there exposed. Gordon Speden tried to cover it up but it was too late, the rust had got to it.[48]

Davey's partners also believed he had negotiated a 20-year lease with the Catholic Church, but it later transpired that he had only been able to get a year-to-year lease. This was hardly a sound basis for a tourism business, but Davey was ever the optimist where leases were concerned.[49]

Chapter Nine

The End of an Era

He used to say that the Hollyford was the land of doing without. It was just a cover-up for the fact that he couldn't afford anything.[1]

To his visitors, Davey Gunn was Lord Hollyford or the Mayor of Martins Bay, and was king of all he surveyed.[2] They, along with his family, assumed that he had secure tenure over 'his land' and was making a good living from the cattle and tourism trips.

The reality was that Davey's livelihood was far from secure, as his family eventually discovered:

> He kept a false front up to the public. He was a poor man in the finish, he had to let everything go. I just put it down to old age, I didn't know his financial exposure, neither did my mother. There wasn't much money there in the finish.[3]

Davey's habit of lighting fires to keep his clearings free of scrub was not winning him any friends in the Forest Service or the Fiordland National Park Board. He had always put a match in any dry bit of bush in the hope that the fire would take hold, and once spent three days at Barrier Flats (with no food or bedding) because the weather was good and he wanted to burn as much as possible.

Davey rather liked fire. In 1949 he inadvertently burnt down one of his sheds (which was full of horse gear) at Martins Bay after throwing a match in a dry bit of bracken on his way out to find some cattle. He once lit a fire under the tail of a bogged cow that was too slow in getting herself out. A Forest Service inspection in February 1953 found that numerous fires had been lit within the last year in state forest and national park land. Five acres of forest had been destroyed on the steep bluffs around the east side of Lake Wilmot but the Forest Service could not establish the cause.[4] The inspector reported:

> Apart from the likelihood of further destruction similar to that already caused, there is a risk of a major conflagration and steps should be taken for all unlicenced [*sic*] burning to be stopped.[5]

In January 1954 the Department of Lands and Survey visited the Hollyford in order to report on whether or not Davey's leases (most of which were due to expire the following month) should be renewed. Their conclusion was that 'there is barely a living in the property',[6] but they also acknowledged that Davey was performing a significant public service:

> While it is recognised that this area in its present state had greater scenic value than it has productive value the fact that Mr Gunn is occupying the country and keeping the tracks open is of considerable value in such a huge area devoid of settlement and it is considered that Mr Gunn should be allowed to lease the Alabaster area for grazing of cattle and that his improvements (Huts) at Alabaster, Lower Pyke, Hidden Falls, Deadmans, Hollyford should be protected by leasing the land immediately surrounding and on which the huts are situated for his lifetime or personal occupancy.[7]

In June 1954 the National Parks Authority approved in principle the incorporation of Davey's pastoral leases in the Hollyford Valley (Runs 471–474: 25,660 acres) into Fiordland National Park. This was about a quarter of the total of his leases and, more importantly, they were the only leases that had not been on a year-to-year basis. Davey managed to achieve a stay of execution for one year, but he was advised that there would be no further extensions.[8]

Three months later the Assistant Commissioner of Crown Lands discussed the matter with Davey and reported:

> This man is not at all happy about his position and has the somewhat mistaken idea that he is more or less being summarily ejected from country which he not only pioneered, but has his whole capital locked up in.

Davey told the Assistant Commissioner that he had spent

Davey at Big Bay during the early 1950s.

Eric Midgley

Happy despite the weather: a tramping party at Hidden Falls, 1953.
Peter Robson

£700 putting through a track from the Lower Pyke to the south side of the Olivine, and that he valued his buildings at £2,000. He also said that his son, Murray, was willing to take over.[9]

Perhaps to add strength to his case Davey persuaded Murray to come into the Hollyford, which he did:

> My father persuaded me to come here. He had great dreams for the Hollyford; they were just dreams, though. I feel sorry for him now – the dreams he had for the place were all undermined by government departments. He didn't [tell us] that the national park had jumped the river and that he only had year-to-year leases and that his cattle were ruined by the deer. He wouldn't let on to my mother. [She] wanted to know why there wasn't much money coming in and he put her off. I only found out when I came here.[10]

Davey's biggest concern was that when the area was added to the national park he wouldn't be allowed to run his guided trips through the area. He was also unsure whether any grazing at all would be allowed within the park. The National Parks Authority initially refused to consider any of these questions:

> . . . it was not prepared to concede these rights in advance to Mr Gunn who had no actual rights in the matter. It was indicated, however, that there would be little doubt that the Authority would give sympathetic consideration to any

Some of Davey's 'treasures' at Deadmans Hut, 1949.
Eric Midgley

reasonable requests by Mr Gunn, in view of his long association with the district.[11]

However, in December 1954 the National Parks Authority approved in principle that Davey be granted a lease over 350 acres of land at the head of Lake Alabaster, and a permit 'over the sites of the huts utilised by him on the tourist tracks maintained by him'.[12]

Davey's other problem was that he was finding it harder and harder to make the cattle pay. Although his stock were of good quality and were sought after at sales, he couldn't raise enough of them, because deer were eating all the feed. In 1951 he brought out 90 sale cattle, a year later it was just 83 beasts, and in 1953 only 74 steers and heifers were brought out.[13]

From the mid-1940s the deer population was completely out of hand.[14] When Eoin Wylie was at the Barrier Flats in 1961 he found a paddock that had been left with the gate shut. The cattle couldn't get in to graze but the deer could. When Wylie rode up, 'There were 400 bloody deer in there. Soon as they saw me, they went out in a wave, a sea of deer jumping over the wire.'[15]

The Department of Lands and Survey report in 1954 recognised the problem: 'The area at Hidden Falls 10 years ago carried 100 head [of cattle] all year and since then deer have been so numerous that it is impossible to run cattle there.'[16]

It is also doubtful that Davey was making much from his guided walks operation. If a trip was advertised it would run, even if there were only one or two people on it. They would pay £10 each but on a 10-day trip the wages for the guide alone would be £10, and there were considerable costs in terms of wages involved in getting supplies to the huts.

Murray could see what was happening:

> He didn't run the tourist side properly either. He was losing money on it . . . I would talk to him about it and say 'You can't keep this 10-day trek up, you've got all these huts to replace'. He didn't take any notice. He just carried on the way he had and he was losing money on it. What drove him was the fact that it brought people here and he liked meeting people all the time.[17]

Davey had hoped that his son would take over both the cattle and the tourism operations, but Murray's arrival in the area heralded a difficult time for them both. Father and son did not know each other well, and Murray hadn't been brought up to a rugged farming life. He was fit and excelled at sports such as badminton and squash, but these were not activities Davey could relate to. Then there was the constant presence of a certain third party: 'He got me here and I was just another labourer. With the influence of Jean Prust I couldn't get close to him, nobody could.'[18]

Murray also had trouble reconciling himself to some of his father's quirks:

Murray Gunn with some of his sporting trophies.
Murray Gunn Collection

When I came here all the huts were cluttered with boxes, tins and other junk. I got armfuls of stuff and put it out the back. When my father got to the hut, he looked around but didn't say anything. The next morning it was threatening rain and Jack Jenkins said to my father, 'We'd better get cracking before the rain comes.' My father said, 'Oh, I have to stay here and clean up.' Anyway we went off and I found out that he had put all the stuff back in the hut. When I saw him he said, 'I didn't like the hut when I first saw it, but I like it now.'[19]

Murray was initially undeterred:

Davey with his daughter Dorothy Parlane and granddaughter Sandra in Wellington, 1953.

Murray Gunn Collection

Hendersons Camp, now known as Hollyford Camp or Gunn's Camp.

Murray Gunn Collection

Another time I was at Big Bay and I had a spare day to tidy up the hut. This time I hid all the boxes where he wouldn't find them. When he turned up there on a muster with Ed Cotter, he opened the door and looked in. He turned to Ed and said, 'This vandalism must stop!' But he didn't say anything to me about it.[20]

It seems that Davey was starting to feel his age. Gordon Speden remembered that sometime during the winter of 1954 Davey talked about retiring to Martins Bay. He told Speden, 'My heart's gone on me.' He later said his doctor had told him it was only indigestion. Davey apparently had it in mind that he was going to muster until he was 70, and then go and live at Martins Bay with Jean. He planned to build a hut near McKenzies and was looking forward to his friends being able to fly in and stay with him there.[21]

Retirement income was naturally an issue, as it is certain Davey intended to go on supporting Ethel. In June 1955 he agreed to sell out 'straight away' to Ed Cotter, Jack Jenkins and Murray. The plan was for Jenkins to handle the cattle side of the business while Cotter and Murray worked the tourism business. Davey left immediately for Wellington, he said, to 'fix up' the lease.[22]

The mystery is what Davey thought he had to sell. He only owned one bush-covered 50-acre section, on the side of Lake McKerrow. The remainder of his 'assets' were leases: one for a 50-acre section leased in perpetuity from the Crown (near the old McKenzie homestead), a lease to 2,000 acres in the Hollyford Valley (in the vicinity of Deadmans) that would expire in one year, a licence to occupy 350 acres at the head of Lake Alabaster, and a year-to-year grazing licence for land at Martins Bay, Big Bay and in the Upper Pyke that was not transferable.

When Davey came back to the Hollyford, no doubt having been put straight on his position, he imposed a whole lot of conditions on the sale. Cotter, Jenkins and Murray felt they couldn't agree to these, and the plan lapsed. Davey then changed his plans, deciding to retire to a hut near Hollyford Camp. Murray, realising that there was little future for him in the Hollyford, left for a position in Invercargill.[23] Jack Jenkins, who was fond of Davey, remained as guide and musterer. Ed Cotter was still keen on developing the tourism potential of the area, and Davey agreed to give him first option on the tourism side of the business should he sell, although Cotter said they never got to the stage of discussing money.

Murray felt sorry for his father, but also felt powerless:

> You could see he was lonely. I saw him on his last muster when I was passing through the Upper Pyke . . . He was back in his shell. It was such a strain on him, he [was] skin and bone in the last few years but he was determined to go on mustering until he was 70.[24]

Davey's last muster was in March 1955, when he brought out 107 beasts to the saleyards at Gore. During the winter he spent time packing stores to the huts in preparation for guided walkers. In the weeks before his death Davey was mustering at Te Anau Downs Station for his friends the Chartres family. He was described as being in excellent spirits and 'for a man of his age was very agile'.[25]

Just before Christmas 1955 Paul Riley, a friend of Davey's and a keen hunter, arrived at Hollyford Camp with 12-year-old Warren Shaw, the son of Riley's cousin Gwen Shaw and her husband Jim. Riley had spent a considerable amount of time in the Hollyford and had offered to help tidy up the airstrip at Martins Bay. Warren, the eldest of four in a close-knit family, was very good at sports (particularly rugby) and had turned down a scout-group camping holiday at Lake Wanaka to come to the Hollyford and learn about hunting.

Davey in April 1955 with a group of trampers about to head to Milford via the Kaipo and Harrison River. From left: Pat Clark (now Turnbull), Davey, Peter Campbell, Steve Miller and Harry Lawson.

Derek and Pat Turnbull Collection

Davey got on well with Riley and was happy to join him and Warren on a trip down the valley. Jack Jenkins, who was going to man the boat on Lake McKerrow during the tourist season, planned to travel down with the party.[26]

On Christmas Day the four left Hollyford Camp at 10 a.m. for Pyke Hut with three packhorses. At Hidden Falls they crossed the Hollyford River and followed a track along the south bank. At about 5 p.m. they reached the 'lower ford', where they would cross the Hollyford to continue on to Pyke. The ford was about 30 metres wide and the current was swift. The water was about a metre deep, which was lower than normal, as there had been no rain for some time.

Jenkins entered the ford first on his horse. Davey mounted his horse, Dick, a six-year-old who was usually reliable and surefooted, and helped Warren up to sit behind him. Riley was a little further back and had only just entered the water when he saw Davey's horse stumble and fall. In typical style, Davey had repaired the saddle with copper wire and rivets, and the girth strap broke when the horse fell.[27] The saddle turned over and Davey's left leg was caught under the horse. While the horse was down in the river it blocked the flow of water so that Warren was able to find his feet and stand up, but as soon as the horse scrambled to his feet the current swept Warren away.

Jack Jenkins at 'The Slip' in
the Kaipo Valley, about 1954.
Ed Cotter

Riley saw him swimming for the far bank, but the current was too strong.

When the horse stood up, Davey was released and was also swept away. Davey had never learnt to swim and may have been injured by the horse, but he was still conscious at this point. Jenkins, who had reached the far bank, ran downstream to try to help, and Riley leapt off his horse and ran down the other side of the river.

Brian Swete was later told what happened next:

> Jack Jenkins, who was quite a strong swimmer, told me that he was running down beside the river trying to keep up. Davey was leaping off the bottom and coming up out of the water. He was roaring like a bull [presumably getting air]. He did that about three times and then he went into white water and Jack couldn't keep up.[28]

Both Davey and Warren had disappeared. The river below the ford was deep, swift and full of snags and, although Jenkins and Riley searched desperately along the sides of the river, it was difficult to see in among the logs from the bank. After two hours, realising there was little chance of finding either victim alive, the two men decided to go for assistance. They rode out to Hollyford Camp and then drove a Land Rover to Te Anau and woke the police constable, William Coll, at 2 a.m.

Riley carried on to Seacliff, near Dunedin, in his Fordson

van to break the news to Warren's family. After a hurried break-fast he got back in the van and drove Warren's father, Jim Shaw, to the Hollyford. Friends and family initially held out hope that Warren, who was strong and fit, would have made it to a river-bank downstream.

Murray Gunn had gone home to Oamaru for Christmas, and he and his mother were woken at 7 a.m. by a policeman who told them about the accident. Murray said Ethel took the news well – 'There was no love lost between them by then.'[29]

Within a couple of hours of being woken, Constable Coll had made up a search party of seven Te Anau residents, 'who readily responded'. They were joined by eight trampers from Hollyford Camp, who had been about to start the round trip. Jean Prust, who was also at Hollyford Camp, organised food and supplies for the searchers, including a search and rescue team that arrived from Invercargill later in the day.

Camps were set up along the river and at Pyke Hut, and the next three days were spent searching for two bodies. Paul Riley and two Australian trampers, Vera Attwater and Pamela Leafe, took turns in the water tied to a piece of rope and searching among the snags below the ford. Each could only manage a few minutes at a time in the ice-cold river.

Paul Riley found Warren's body at 9 a.m. on 29 December, 150 metres downstream from the ford, stuck in some tangled stumps where the water was about six metres deep. The body was caught too far below the surface for anyone to retrieve it, but after several hours work by Jenkins, Riley and Attwater, 'at great personal risk', a rope was attached to the body and it was dislodged and brought ashore at 4.15 p.m.[30]

The search for Davey's body continued for several days. Murray arrived from Oamaru, and remembered that many of Davey's old friends turned up to help – if anything, there were too many searchers. The search was eventually called off at 11 a.m. on 30 December.

Davey's friend George Burnby recalled later that he didn't really want to find the body. Davey had always said that if he went missing he didn't want people to look for him, and Burnby was certain Davey would not have wanted to be carted out and buried in Oamaru or Waimate. He would have wanted to stay in his beloved Hollyford.[31]

Warren William Shaw (1943–55) with his dog, Lassie.
Dorothy Andrews

Davey with his horse Dick, who stumbled while fording the Hollyford River on Christmas Day 1955.

Derek and Pat Turnbull Collection

Much later, Murray was able to be philosophical about his father's death:

> What he'd gone through and the way he'd been treated, he had nothing to look forward to in life, the drowning was a blessing in some ways. I felt sorry for him. He lived in a dream world. He thought he could open up the Olivine for cattle and it was impossible. Everything was let go, all the huts had been let go and they weren't suitable for the modern age.[32]

Davey Gunn's body was never found.

Chapter Ten

Davey's Legacy

His spirit lingers on in the tales that are told.[1]

Davey Gunn's death came as a shock to many. He had been in the Hollyford for as long as most people could remember, and although he had begun to show signs of his age, he had always seemed durable, having survived many life-threatening accidents. Davey had become a permanent fixture of the area — when people thought of the Hollyford they thought of Davey.

Elsie Morton echoed the thoughts of many:

> Dave's death is something I just can't seem to realise, even yet. As one of the newspaper accounts put it, he seemed to be 'indestructible'. It just doesn't bear thinking of. So unnecessary, so cruelly unlucky at a time when the river was low.[2]

Newspaper accounts of the drownings often included a tribute to Davey and his achievements. An Invercargill paper noted that Davey would be remembered for two great feats: the 'astonishing' journey he made to get help for the injured after the plane crash at Big Bay in 1936, and for opening up the Hollyford area to trampers and riders. The *Waimate Times* floated the possibility of a memorial cairn. The *New Zealand Free Lance* carried the headline 'The Last of Hollyford's Fabulous Davie Gunn', and the *Weekly News* reported: 'Giant of the Outback: Death Claims Davy Gunn'.[3]

Davey's death was noted in many tramping newsletters around the country. He was held in extraordinary affection by many people who, although they knew him only briefly, had been impressed with his friendliness, his generosity and by the hardy life he lived in the back country.

The author at Davey's memorial cairn at Lower Pyke on Christmas Day 2005, the 50th anniversary of his death. The cairn was erected a year or so after Davey's death by Jean Prust and Alice and Harry Turnbull.
Eddie Newman

Warren Shaw was buried by his family at Warrington cemetery near Dunedin. They had to deal not only with their profound grief but also with the fact that their loss was overshadowed by the death of a much more well-known figure. Many newspaper accounts didn't mention the death of Warren, or only mentioned that 'a boy' had also drowned.

The inquest into the deaths of Warren Shaw and Davey Gunn was opened on 30 December 1955, but the inquest for Davey was adjourned and finally held in Invercargill on 17 May 1956, with evidence being given by Paul Riley, Jack Jenkins and Constable William Coll. Following the finding that Davey had drowned, his death was officially registered and his estate could now be settled.[4] This was initially valued by the Public Trustee at £11,740, which was rather astounding considering that all Davey actually owned was a 50-acre section on the shores of Lake McKerrow.

The rest of Davey's kingdom was leasehold, and letters passed back and forth for some time between the Public Trustee and the Departments of Lands and Survey, the Forest Service and the Fiordland National Park Board as the trustee tried to establish the true value of Davey's estate.

Runs 471–474 were already part of Fiordland National Park, and there was only six months left on the lease of 2,000 acres near Deadmans. Davey was still leasing 71,000 acres at Martins Bay, Big Bay and the Pyke Valley from the Forest

Service, and 350 acres at the head of Lake Alabaster from the Fiordland National Park Board, but both on year-to-year leases. Davey had bequeathed his grazing licences, but the Forest Service pointed out that this transfer needed to be approved by the relevant minister of the Crown.[5]

It was soon apparent that in order for the estate to realise any money at all, Davey's main asset, his cattle, would have to be sold. There were thought to be about 380 of them. To this end the estate applied for, and was granted, a temporary extension of the leases at Martins Bay, Big Bay and the 2,000 acres near Deadmans so the cattle could be mustered and driven out to the saleyards.[6]

There was also some confusion over who owned the huts that Davey had built. The Forest Service head office suggested that it had ownership and that Davey's estate should be charged for any use made of them, but Davey had friends in the Forest Service, and this idea was soon dropped.[7]

The state of Davey's finances (the estate eventually realised perhaps about £2,000) came as a shock to his family. It was fortunate that Ethel's sister Tilly had left Ethel her house when she died, and that Ethel was now in receipt of a pension.

Murray left his position at the Southland County Council and moved to Hollyford Camp in order to help sort out his father's affairs. Jack Jenkins, who was soon to be married to one of the Australians who had helped in the search for Warren's and Davey's bodies, was keen to stay in the area, as was Jean Prust. Jean was a very private person who would not have shown her grief in public and, as the couple's relationship was a secret, it would have been difficult for her to do so. Initially, Jean stayed in a hut near Hollyford Camp that Davey had moved in preparation for his retirement, but she and Murray did not get along, so she soon moved on.[8]

Davey's dogs were bereft. Tim, Davey's constant companion, had been left behind at Hollyford Camp on Davey's final journey because he had cut paws. For six weeks Tim kept a vigil for his beloved owner, and would sit for hours looking down the road in the hope that he would appear. When Jack Jenkins got the nod to muster Davey's cattle he took Tim with him. The dog continued to look for Davey but eventually seemed reconciled to his loss.[9]

Murray was interested in developing the tourism potential of the area but not particularly interested in the cattle. Jenkins was instructed to muster as many as he could for the estate. He undertook musters in 1956 and 1957, but Murray believed he was deliberately leaving breeding cows and young cattle behind. In 1957 Jack attempted to buy the remaining cattle, but Murray refused to sell.[10]

By May 1958 the Department of Crown Lands was complaining about the number of cattle still on its land. If they were not removed by the time the lease expired in a year, the Forest Service would be asked to exterminate them.[11]

Murray organised a group of five musterers to get out as many cattle as they could. They set out in February 1959. Terry Smyth was riding Dick, the horse that had stumbled in the ford on Christmas Day 1955; Bob Healy (Terry's uncle) was riding George; Brian Waddell was riding Chief; Alan Weir was on one of Davey's geldings; and Ruth, Brian's wife, was riding a horse they had bought for dog tucker but decided to keep. Murray accompanied the party to Martins Bay, where they camped in a whitebaiter's hut rather than in Davey's now dilapidated building. After sharing some local knowledge with the musterers, Murray left them to get on with it.

A few days later three fishermen arrived. They had brought with them an outboard motor for the whitebaiter's dinghy and agreed to take Weir, Smyth and Healy across the Hollyford River so they could muster in the Kaipo Valley. Ruth and Brian Waddell stayed behind to fix some fences at Martins Bay before the muster began there. It was a sunny day when Weir and

Musterers with cattle on Big Bay beach.
Ruth and Brian Waddell

The mustering party that set out for Martins Bay in February 1959. Only three of the five would return.
Ruth and Brian Waddell

Smyth arrived back at Martins Bay beach with a mob of cattle and, probably thinking to save time, decided to cross opposite Jerusalem Creek. Bob Healy, who was acting as packer, was several hours behind them.

Ruth and Brian, hearing the dogs, went out to the river to investigate. Both knew it was the wrong place to cross – Murray had warned them – and they yelled for the men to turn back. Too late. The horses soon began to get into difficulty. Ruth and Brian yelled at the men to grab the horses' tails and cried in frustration, powerless to help without a dinghy. The two men disappeared amid a confusion of cattle, dogs and horses. Ruth recalled:

> It was awful, you knew you couldn't save them. Brian was getting out of his clothes but you couldn't swim in that mighty river. We couldn't see what was happening. As soon as the dogs stopped barking, the cattle went back to the beach and took off. And oh my God, all we could see was a black hat floating down the river.[12]

The fishermen were further up the river in the dinghy and responded quickly after hearing two gunshots, indicating that a boat was required, and then a further three, which meant it was urgent. They searched extensively but found no sign of the men.

There was nothing else to do but report the chilling news over the whitebaiter's radio. A plane would be in the following day.

The search for the bodies lasted 16 days. Alan Weir's body was recovered, but Terry Smyth's was never found.[13]

Weir's brother Dave flew in to help with the muster, along with Alan Parker and Ray Paul. By now the muster was running behind and it was doubtful whether they would make it to the sale in time. On 2 March the group left Martins Bay with 130 head of cattle. At Big Bay the yards broke during the night, necessitating an extra day of mustering to retrieve the cattle. Then, at Barrier Hut, the mustering party was subjected to torrential rain. One of the musterers woke in the night with a heavy weight on his leg. Realising it was his dog, he kicked it off smartly but was surprised when it landed with a splash. Turning on his torch, he saw that there was 15 centimetres of water running through the hut.

From Pyke Hut the going was easier and the musterers reached Hollyford Camp on 16 March, an exhausting six weeks after they had set out. They had managed to get out 120 of the 130 cattle they started with, but they had lost eight dogs along the way and had to shoot a horse that fell off the track around Lake Wilmot. The cattle were trucked to Lorneville but, as they had missed the main sale, the price they fetched was not high. It was a disappointing end to a muster that had cost two lives and considerable mental anguish and physical hardship.[14]

The fate of the various missing dogs was uncertain, as the national park ranger later reported:

> On the last muster, where there seemed to be nearly as many dogs as there were cattle, several of the cattle escaped and signs of them have been noted recently near Swamp Creek . . . there is no certainty as to the whereabouts of some of the dogs lost in the Park, enroute. One was destroyed (unapproachable) at Homer Tunnel in June. Another was seen later near High Falls Creek [Humboldt Creek]. Yet another was reported in the Lake Howden area.[15]

Various sympathetic individuals within the Forest Service had the lease extended for another two years (to 30 April 1962) so that the remaining cattle could be brought out. That date came and went, but the Forest Service delayed taking 'positive action' in order to give Murray 'every opportunity of organising a final muster'.[16]

Not long after the lease expired, the estate finally found someone who was willing to consider rounding up the remaining cattle. Eoin Wylie, an experienced 22-year-old musterer from Lake Wakatipu, rode in during the winter of 1962 to have a look, and submitted a tender. The estate agreed to pay him 30 per cent of the price obtained for any cattle that were sold. Wylie convinced his mate Les Wade to join him, and in the spring the pair set off from Hollyford Camp with seven horses and two dog teams. They travelled up the Pyke to Big Bay, where they met Jack Jenkins, who was whitebaiting. Jenkins gave them some advice, warning them not to cross the Hollyford River near Jerusalem Creek because that's where two of the last musterers had drowned. Wylie remembered later that he said, 'Oh yeah, I'll watch out for that,' but 'it went in one ear and out the other'.[17]

After spending nearly a month fixing the yards at Martins Bay they headed down to the Kaipo. They found the cattle there too wild, so they didn't bother to muster them, but they got 'a good call' at McKenzies. They took the cattle down to the beach and tried to get them up to the crossing. Wylie recalled:

> We couldn't get them up there – they took off and stampeded down the sand and started to swim across the estuary and we thought we might as well let them go. The cattle got to the other side and went into the bush with the dogs on them. We thought if the cattle can get across, then so can we.

Les Wade at Martins Bay.
Garth King

Eoin Wylie on Chief,
Martins Bay.
Eoin Wylie

Both men had apparently forgotten Jack Jenkins's warning.

Wylie was riding an old horse of Davey's, Chief, which wouldn't enter the water. Les Wade was riding a young horse that went in without hesitation.

> What we didn't know was that the river's got two currents –
> the big river running like hell at the top and the tide roaring
> in underneath. When cattle swim they swim high but when
> a horse goes in his back comes down and he gets tugged over
> backwards by the bottom current. Les's horse went end over
> end and Les got smacked on the head. All I could see was
> this body floating down the river.[18]

Some fishermen who had arrived in the men's absence heard the cattle and dogs and came out to see what was going on. Seeing Wylie running down the opposite side of the river desperately trying to reach something, they jumped into the dinghy, started the outboard motor and sped across. By the time they reached Wade he was only semi-conscious and couldn't swim; he was getting into the stronger current near the river mouth. It was a very close thing.

The two musterers took a break for Christmas, but the trustees of Davey's estate were getting impatient and demanded that the men bring some cattle out immediately. The men rounded up about 50 cattle and set out. It was a quick trip – 10

A chip off the old block: Murray Gunn at Hollyford Camp.

Gordon Speden Collection

days – to Hollyford Camp but there were losses along the way, including 'difficult' cattle that had to be shot, and the two men arrived out with only 24 cattle.[19]

In January 1966 the Forest Service, having finally run out of patience, gave the trustees one month to remove the remaining cattle or they would be destroyed. The estate responded by relinquishing any claim on the cattle, whose numbers were gradually reduced over the following years by hunters and commercial fishermen based in the area.[20]

Meanwhile, Murray was trying to get to grips with the tourism operation, but because Davey had no rights or concessions in law, this was a difficult task. Murray had very limited capital, but money was desperately needed to upgrade the facilities. Eventually, he succeeded in obtaining a formal lease for six of his father's hut sites, but soon after, a jetboat he had organised for the Hollyford River sank while being taken into the river mouth. Murray could not afford the cost of salvage so the boat was sold.[21] At this point Murray, having run out of funds, had to relinquish the lease.

This left the way clear for Ed Cotter, who had not forgotten the Hollyford. Cotter started Adventours in 1965, offering a five-day tour that included launch and jetboat trips, with the option of flying out. Unfortunately, the concession was granted only seven weeks before the season began, so that Cotter's new lodges were not finished and there had not been time to fly in adequate food supplies. Consequently, the brochure oversold the tours and there were many complaints. By 1968 Adventours had closed down.[22]

The next attempt was by Viv Allot and Jules Tapper (both of Invercargill), in partnership with Murray Gunn. Hollyford Tourist and Travel Company started in 1968 and built on the concept started by Ed Cotter. Their 21-foot launch on the lake was named the *Davey Gunn* and they used two V-nosed alloy jet-boats on the rivers – the first time this kind of craft had been used commercially in New Zealand. The company offered a five-day walk in/walk out trip, or a four-day walk in/fly out option. This operation continues successfully today, having changed hands in 1996 and 2003.[23] Murray was only involved for the first year or

A jetboat carrying trampers on the Hollyford River, in about 1966. The driver is Jack Jordan.
Ed Cotter

so, leaving after some differences of opinion to concentrate his energy on developing Hollyford Camp.

After Davey's death his story refused to die. The plaque at Marian Corner alerted the many thousands of people who travelled along the road to Milford of Davey's 'heroic journey', and tourism guides, books and newspaper articles continued to recite the details.

Elsie K. Morton wrote glowing accounts of the Hollyford and of Davey. In 1957 he featured in her article 'Fiordland's Trinity of Mighty Men' in the *Weekly News*. Every now and then articles would re-tell the story of Davey's race from Big Bay, with headlines such as 'Thrilling Rescue Followed Crash' and 'Davie Became a Legend'. Murray further promoted the legend when he set up an exhibition of pioneering artefacts from Martins Bay at the Wakatipu centennial celebrations in Queenstown in 1962.[24]

Murray Gunn never married, instead devoting his life to Hollyford Camp, where he established a museum containing objects, information and photos of his father's time in the area. Despite their troubled relationship, it has been Murray who has done most to keep his father's memory alive. At the camp there are plenty of reminders of 'the land of doing without', and Murray has even commemorated some of Davey's horses in the names of the cabins. Murray has become a character in his own

Murray Gunn in 2003 with the saddle his father was using when his horse stumbled in the river.
Julia Bradshaw

Ruth McClintock (née Benstead) and Emma Speden at Hollyford Camp in the 1970s.

Gordon Speden Collection

right and numerous articles have been written about him. His quirky sense of humour and dry wit have long alternately terrified and delighted tourists. In 2005 ill-health forced his reluctant move to Te Anau, and Hollyford Camp is now administered by the Hollyford Museum Charitable Trust.

After leaving the Hollyford, Jean Prust spent some time at Te Anau Downs Station before returning to nursing, first at Lawrence Hospital and later at St George's Hospital, Christchurch. She maintained her links with Big Bay whitebaiters Eric and Daphne Midgley and attended Jack Jenkins's funeral in 1987. Jean retired to Lyttelton and in 1992 described the Hollyford as 'one of the highlights of my life'. She died in 1995 at the age of 84.[25] She never married.

Jack Jenkins took some time to come to terms with Davey's death, having been there at the time and been unable to help. He was similar to Davey in many ways, and Brian Swete believed Jenkins was closer to Davey than anyone. Until his death he continued to visit Big Bay at least once a year to catch whitebait.[26]

Ruth Benstead eventually married in 1960, aged 56. She and her husband, John McClintock, were very happy, and Ruth told Murray it was wonderful to be married. She visited the Hollyford again in the 1970s, with her friends Gordon and Emma Speden.[27]

Davey was survived by Ethel and by two of his sisters, Gus

Deadmans Hut in the 1970s. Soon after, the river washed away the ruins of the hut.

Gordon Speden Collection

(Sarah Augusta) and Jean, and his brother Bob. Ethel continued to live in Oamaru and finally visited the Hollyford for the first time shortly before she died, in February 1962. Davey's daughter Dorothy visited the Hollyford several times, but her sister Isabel first went to Hollyford Camp in May 1999, to visit Murray.[28]

Two books about Davey's cattle musters were written after his death. Rupert Sharpe, well known to *New Zealand Weekly News* readers from the 1930s as 'R.D.S.', travelled to the Hollyford to met Davey, of whom he had heard several accounts. Davey invited him to join the next muster, and Sharpe's very readable account of this trip was published posthumously as *Fiordland Muster.*[29]

Gordon Donaldson-Law was a 39-year-old Englishman working for the Don Cossack Riders as a showman performing dangerous 'tricks' on horses when he discovered the Hollyford. After he read Gerry Hamilton's account of a muster in the *Wide World Magazine*, he wrote to Davey asking for a job. Receiving a positive reply six months later, he immediately sailed for New Zealand and spent nine months of 1948 working in the Hollyford. *Hollyford Muster 1948* was published a few months after his death in 1995.[30]

Jean Prust, feeling that Davey needed a tribute, wrote a 40-page manuscript titled 'Gunn of the Hollyford' sometime during the early 1960s. Its concluding words were a heartfelt compliment; 'Davey's dauntless courage about which he was so matter of fact, is not common. He was a Man.'[31]

Davey's story inspired several songs and at least one poem. Dusty Spittle, who grew up on a farm near Gore, never met Davey but had heard about him. Dusty's father knew Jim Speden, who had worked for Davey and was a great story-teller: the family heard many tales of the Hollyford. Dusty admired cowboys, and Davey was one of his heroes. He also knew the Waddells and heard more Hollyford stories from them. In the mid-1960s Dusty was working in Australia and began writing songs, one of the first being 'Old Davey Gunn', which he recorded in the 1970s. His many live performances always include a few Hollyford tales, helping to keep the legend alive.[32]

Joe Charles wrote two songs about Davey: 'Davey Gunn' about the plane crash at Big Bay, and another (confusingly) called 'Davy Gunn', about cattle droving. This latter finishes:

Oh, Davy Gunn, his work is done,
For lost and drowned is he;
And though his bones lie 'neath the stones,
His memory always dwells,
By cattle tracks and lonely shacks,
Where the bushman sings and yells.[33]

There are no longer any cattle tracks, shacks or bushmen in the Hollyford, but Joe Charles caught the right tone in his tribute to Davey, whose exploits still captivate visitors to the Hollyford, and many others besides.

In some ways Davey could be seen as having failed in the Hollyford. He lost the battle to run cattle in the area; he lost the battle against deer. While he built up a tourism business, it badly needed capital investment and he simply did not have it. Financially he finished with almost nothing.

But in so many other ways Davey succeeded. He achieved what many aim for: he lived in a place he loved and worked at what he enjoyed doing. He could organise his time to suit himself, and he helped put Fiordland on the map.

Much of Davey's legacy was the subtle impact he had on people and their actions. Many people's lives were changed or their horizons expanded by their visit to the Hollyford and their interaction with Davey. Elisabeth Stuart-Jones was one tramper who attested to that:

The experience of this trip, recommended to me by an elderly sister at the Hutt Hospital, proved life changing and [was] the forerunner of many subsequent tramping trips throughout the South Island of New Zealand. I feel very privileged in retrospect to have seen the wild unspoilt Fiordland forest . . . before eco-tourism got hold of it and ironed out all the wrinkles and struggles . . . that we experienced and were changed by in 1951.[34]

If the McKenzies' runs had been taken over by someone who was in it purely for 'a good spec', they would soon have been abandoned. The tracks would have quickly become overgrown and the huts dilapidated.

Davey took over the runs and kept them going for almost 30 years, kept the tracks open and maintained the huts. The track is now hugely popular with guided and independent walkers, and offers a special opportunity to follow a river from the Southern Alps to the sea. The track through the Pyke Valley has become overgrown, although 10–20 parties a year battle their way through. Davey's huts are long gone, his cattle yards have fallen down and his clearings are overgrown. But the Hollyford is still a destination, and still changes the lives of people who visit.

Davey would have liked that.

Notes

Chapter One

1. Peter Newton, *Sixty Thousand on the Hoof*, A. H. & A. W. Reed, Wellington, 1975, p. 219.
2. Copy of registration of birth, 1888/4141, Registrar of Births, Deaths & Marriages, Lower Hutt. Note: The 1888 registration is an amended entry; the first registration (1887/4217) is unavailable for viewing. Kathryn Johan Jones, Gunn Family History, Murray Gunn Collection.
3. Stones Directory Otago/Southland, 1909, 1915. Jean Prust, 'Gunn of the Hollyford', unpub. manuscript, copies held by Julia Bradshaw, Murray Gunn and Hocken Library (Barlow Papers, MS-1416/103) but original not located, p. 1. NZ Defence Force, Personnel Archives, David John Gunn, registration no. 84378, now held by Archives NZ, Wellington. Murray Gunn, interviewed by author, January 2003.
4. Mortgage documents, DAAB D116 130-51228, Archives NZ, Dunedin. H. M. Thompson, *East of the Rock and Pillar: History of Strath Taieri and Macraes district*, Capper Press, 1977, p. 187. Peter Marshall, written comm. to author, 14 June 2003.
5. Gordon Parry, *N.M.A. The story of the first 100 years: The National Mortgage and Agency Company of NZ Limited 1864–1964*, National Mortgage and Agency Co. of New Zealand, Dunedin, 1964, pp. 150–51.
6. Annual Sheep Owner Returns, *AJHR*, H-23b, 1920–26. George Burnby, interviewed by author, April 2003.
7. Isabel Findlay, interviewed by author, 1 September 2004. Confirmed by Doug Gunn.
8. Runs Register, c. 1878–c.1960, DAAK D84 768, Archives NZ, Dunedin.
9. Isabel Findlay, interviewed by author, 1 September 2004, confirmed by Doug Gunn.
10. Doug Gunn, interviewed by author, 28 August 2004. Isabel Findlay, interviewed by author, 1 September 2004.
11. Obituary in *Oamaru Mail*, 10 August 1938. Stones Otago/Southland Directory 1921, 1926. Also unsourced newspaper article about Willetts Tea Rooms, 10 January 1996, Murray Gunn Collection.
12. Lands and Survey files: DAFU D311 168q-M345, DAAK D84 584b-ML3022, Archives NZ, Dunedin.
13. The transfer was dated 14 July 1926, Runs Register, c.1878–c.1960, op. cit.
14. *Lake Wakatip Mail*, 24 August 1926.
15. R. H. Hooker, *The Archaeology of South Westland Maori*, NZ Forest Service, Hokitika, 1986, pp. 45–48. John Hall Jones, *Martins Bay*, Craig Printing, 1988, pp. 39, 45–48. Paul Madgwick, *Aotea: A history of the South Westland Maori*, printed by Greymouth Evening Star, 1992, pp. 102–04.
16. *West Coast Times*, 3 January 1871, p. 2. *Wise's New Zealand Directory*, 1898.
17. Runs Register, c.1878–c.1960, op. cit. *Lake Wakatip Mail*, 1 November 1910. Hall Jones, *Martins Bay*, pp. 89–90.
18. Laura C. Kroetsch, 'Fine in the Morning: The life writing of Alice McKenzie', MA thesis, 1994, Victoria University of Wellington, p. 44. Runs Register, c.1878–c.1960, op. cit.
19. Newton, *Sixty Thousand*, p. 219. List of stock included in the draft of a partnership agreement between Roderick MacKenzie and son and the McKenzie Brothers of Martins Bay, dated May 1923, Gordon Speden Collection (the agreement was never finalised).
20. 'Martins Bay: Down the Hollyford Valley', *Otago Daily Times*, 28 March 1916, p. 6. Samuel Turner, *Conquest of the Southern Alps*, Fisher & Unwin, London, 1922, p. 259.
21. Copy of a memorandum from the Conservator of Forests in Invercargill to the Director of the State Forest Service in Wellington, 16 December 1927, held by Murray Gunn, original source not known.
22. Copy of final notice issued for lease ML3022 for runs 492 and 495 by Department of Lands and Survey Dunedin, 20 April 1926, Murray Gunn Collection.

23. 'The Wild West: Return of Messrs McKenzie Bros. and W. Beer', newspaper article dated 10 June 1926, almost certainly from *Lake Wakatip Mail*, author's collection.

24. Copy of a memorandum from the Conservator of Forests, op. cit.

25. Isabel Findlay, interviewed by author, 1 September 2004. Confirmed by Doug Gunn.

26. NZ Defence Force, Personnel Archives, Patrick William Fraser, AABK 18805 W5515, box 20, Archives NZ, Wellington.

27. Marriage registration for Patrick Fraser and Dempster Johnston, 1907/3969, Registrar of Births, Deaths & Marriages, Lower Hutt. Birth registration for (Patrick) William Fraser, 1882, Oamaru, courtesy of Oamaru branch, NZ Society of Genealogists

28. Draft Tongariro National Park Management Plan, January 2003, Department of Conservation, p. 6: www.doc.govt.nz/Explore/001~National-Parks/ Fiordland-National-Park/Fiordland-National-Park-General-Information.asp

29. Runs Register, c.1878–c.1960, op. cit.

30. George M. Moir, *Guide Book to the Tourist Routes of the Great Southern Lakes and Fiords of Western Otago*, ODT & Witness Newspapers Co., 1925, pp. 53–54. David R. Jennings, 'Down the Hollyford', *Southland Times*, 6 May 1939, in W. Vance Papers, MS-Papers-111-11, Alexander Turnbull Library, Wellington.

31. Eric James, *Hokitika Guardian*, 3 July 1929, p. 2. NZ State Forest Service Report on S.F. 24 and 25, June 1932, in Forest Service Timber Utilisation File, F1, W3129, 138, 15/6/7a, part 1, Archives NZ, Wellington.

32. Newton, *Sixty Thousand*, p. 219.

33. Prust, 'Gunn of the Hollyford', p. 32. W. A. Anderson, *Doctor in the Mountains*, A. H. & A. W. Reed, Wellington, 1967, pp. 77–78. Doug Gunn, interviewed by author, 28 August 2004.

34. Anderson, *Doctor*, p. 77.

35. Prust, 'Gunn of the Hollyford', p. 32. Anderson, *Doctor*, pp. 77–78.

36. Dorothy Parlane, written comm. to author, December 2003.

37. Lands and Survey file: DAFU D311 168q-M345, op. cit.

38. NZ Defence Force, Personnel Archives, Patrick William Fraser, op. cit.

39. Copy of lease agreement, courtesy of Mrs Margaret Leaker, Christchurch.

Chapter Two

1. Grazing Licences and Leases, Southland Conservancy, M. A./D. J. Gunn, Martins Bay Survey District etc, file: F1 W3219 38/7/25/1, box 245, Archives NZ, Wellington.

2. T. B. Richardson, 'Legendary Man of the Hills . . .', *Southland Daily News*, 15 November 1947, p. 10. Eric James in *Hokitika Guardian*, 3 July 1929, p. 2. Eric James, 'Exploration in Unknown Otago: part II (Over the Red Mountains)', *Otago Daily Times*, c.28 August 1930; and 'part III (Still Southward)', *Otago Daily Times*, 4 September 1930. Also *Stone's Directories Otago/Southland*, 1933–36.

3. Doug Gunn, interviewed by author, 28 August 2004.

4. Ibid.

5. James, 'Exploration in Unknown Otago'.

6. David R. Jennings, 'Down the Hollyford', *Southland Times*, 6 May 1939, part of W. Vance Papers, MS-Papers-111-11, Alexander Turnbull Library, Wellington.

7. James in *Hokitika Guardian*, 3 July 1929, p. 2.

8. Daphne Midgley, interviewed by author, 8 July 2005.

9. Southland Conservator of Forests, M. J. Dolomer, to Westland Conservator, 2 February 1934, file: F1 W3129 38/7/25/1, box 245, Archives NZ, Wellington.

10. Memo, Conservator of Forests, Invercargill, to Director of the State Forest Service in Wellington, 16 December 1927, held by Murray Gunn, original source not known. Grazing Licences and Leases, Southland Conservancy, op. cit.

11. Runs Register, c.1878–c.1960, DAAK D84 768, Archives NZ, Dunedin.

12. James in *Hokitika Guardian*, 3 July 1929, p. 2.

13. Ibid.

14. Murray Gunn, interviewed by author, January 2003.

15. Lands and Survey file: DAAK D84 584b-ML3022, Archives NZ, Dunedin.

16. Ibid. 'The Last of Hollyford's Fabulous Davey Gunn', *Free Lance*, January 1956, Murray Gunn Collection. F. J. Lucas, *Popeye Lucas, Queenstown*, A. H. & A. W. Reed, Wellington, 1968, p. 125.

17. Information from scrapbook, supplied by Lindsay McCurdy's daughter, Mrs Mary Thomson, Waimate.

18. Lake County Council rates books, Lakes District Museum, Arrowtown.

19. Lands and Survey file: DAFU D311 168q-M345, Archives NZ, Dunedin.

20. Commissioner of Crown Lands, Dunedin, to D. J. Gunn, 2 February 1933, ibid.

21. Commissioner of Crown Lands, Dunedin, to D. J.

Gunn, 15 December 1933, ibid. Grazing Licences and Leases, Southland Conservancy, op cit.

22. Letter from Commissioner of Crown Lands, ibid.

23. *New Zealand Yearbook 1936*, Government Printer, 1935, p. 595.

24. Lands and Survey file: DAFU D311 168q-M345, op. cit. Information about payment of £3 per week from Murray Gunn.

25. Murray Gunn, interviewed by author, January 2003.

26. Lands and Survey file: DAFU D311 168q-M345, op. cit.

27. Harold J. Anderson, *Men of the Milford Road*, Craig Printing Co., 1985 (2nd edn), p. 27.

28. 'The Wild West Coast', unsourced newspaper article, 10 June 1926, probably from *Lake Wakatip Mail*. *Otago Daily Times*, 28 March 1916.

29. Conservator of Forests, Invercargill, to Conservator of Forests, Hokitika, 2 February 1934, Grazing Licences and Leases, Southland Conservancy, op cit.

30. C. M. Todd, 'Red Mountain and the Limbo Valley', *New Zealand Alpine Journal*, Vol. 14, No. 9, 1952, p. 257, quoting private comm. with D. Gunn, 1952. Thomas Macdonald to the Minister of Internal Affairs, 18 August 1947, file: Te Anau Lake Wakatipu Track, TO 1 38/51, part 4, Archives NZ, Wellington. Alex Dickie, 'From the Hollyford to the Arawata', *New Zealand Alpine Journal*, 1934, Vol. 5, pp. 307–09. Noted by Lindsay McCurdy in his account of a trip into that area in August 1934, courtesy of Ann Irving, Invercargill.

31. Noted by Lindsay McCurdy, ibid. D. Le H. M., 'Riding Down the Lower Hollyford', *Outdoors* (Otago Tramping Club magazine), June 1937, Vol. 3, No. 4.

32. Jennings, 'Journey Down the Hollyford', *Southland Times*, 13 May 1939, p. 13.

33. Jean Prust, 'Gunn of the Hollyford', unpublished manuscript, copies held by Julia Bradshaw, Murray Gunn and Hocken Library (Barlow Papers, MS-1416/103) but original not located, p. 28. Confirmed by Doug Gunn, interviewed by author, 8 July 2005.

34. Diary of David McDonald, copy courtesy of the late David McDonald, Dunedin.

35. John Hall Jones, *Martins Bay*, Craig Printing Co., 1988, pp. 108–11.

36. Diary of David McDonald.

37. Arthur Bradshaw, *Flying by Bradshaw: Memoirs of a pioneer pilot 1933–1975*, ed. David Phillips and Graeme McConnell, Proctor Publications, 2000, p. 69.

38. Copy of grazing licence held by Murray Gunn.

39. D. J. Gunn to Commissioner of Crown Lands, 28 November 1934, Murray Gunn Collection.

40. Conservator of Forests, Invercargill, to D. J. Gunn, 3 January 1935, copy held by Ian Speden, Wellington.

41. Grazing Licences and Leases, Southland Conservancy, op. cit. Conservator of Forests to Commissioner of Crown Lands, 11 February 1954, file: DAFU D324 47a/4/20, Archives NZ, Dunedin. Apparently after Davey's death the authorities were surprised to find that there were cattle in the Kaipo valley: Murray Gunn, interviewed by author, January 2003.

42. Dorothy Parlane, written comm. to author, December 2003.

43. Elfin Mcdonald (née Shaw), pers. comm. to author, November 2004.

44. Murray Gunn, interviewed by author, January 2003.

Chapter Three

1. Jack Jenkins's description of Davey Gunn as recounted to author by Brian Swete, 14 June 1993.

2. NZ Defence Force, Personnel Archives, David John Gunn, registration number 84378, now held by Archives NZ, Wellington. Olga Sansom, 'Davey Gunn of the Hollyford', *New Zealand Listener*, 11 September 1959, p. 5. W. B. Beattie, Bill Beattie's New Zealand, Hodder & Stoughton, Auckland, 1970, pp. 47–48.

3. Gordon Speden, obituary for David John Gunn, Gordon Speden Collection. An edited version appeared in the *New Zealand Alpine Journal*, 1956.

4. Murray Gunn, interviewed by author, January 2003.

5. Doug Gunn, interviewed by author, 28 August 2004.

6. There are no photos that show Davey with a beard. Jean Prust, 'Gunn of the Hollyford', unpublished manuscript, copies held by Julia Bradshaw, Murray Gunn and Hocken Library (Barlow Papers, MS-1416/103) but original not located, p. 16. 'The Last of the Hollyford's Fabulous Davey Gunn', *Free Lance*, January 1956, Murray Gunn Collection. Obituary in *Tararua Tramper*, February 1956, p. 8.

7. Prust, 'Gunn of the Hollyford', p. 5.

8. Probably J. H. Walton, editor of *Southland Tramper: 50th Jubilee Edition 1947–1997*, Southland Tramping Club, c.1998.

9. Prust, 'Gunn of the Hollyford', p. 3.

10. Ibid., p. 1. Doug Gunn, interviewed by author, 28 August 2004.

11. Murray Gunn, interviewed by author, January 2003.
12. Rupert Sharpe, *Fiordland Muster*, Hodder and Stoughton, London, 1966, pp. 95–96.
13. Ibid., p. 77.
14. Ibid., pp. 92–93.
15. Alan Snook, phone conversation with author, 25 September 2005.
16. Murray Gunn, interviewed by Morag Forrester, 31 May 2000.
17. Ibid.
18. Sharpe, *Fiordland Muster*, pp. 93–94.
19. Prust, 'Gunn of the Hollyford', p. 4. Gordon Donaldson-Law, *Hollyford Muster 1948*, Sylvia Donaldson-Law, Nelson, 1995, p. 16. Alan De La Mare, interviewed by author, 1992.
20. Jean Greenslade, interviewed by author, 30 January 1994. Murray Gunn, interviewed by author, January 2003. Prust, 'Gunn of the Hollyford', p. 4.
21. Ibid.
22. Doug Gunn, interviewed by author, 28 August 2004, Doug Gunn, written comments on Rupert Sharpe's account, Murray Gunn Collection.
23. Sharpe, *Fiordland Muster*, pp. 71–72.
24. Ray Wilson, interviewed by Jack Perkins, c.1990, 97/120, BC92/34, Sound Archives Nga Taonga Korero, Christchurch. Prust, 'Gunn of the Hollyford', p. 31.
25. Ian Haggitt, interviewed by author, 26 April 1994.
26. Ray Wilson, interviewed by Jack Perkins, c.1990, op. cit.
27. Murray Gunn, interviewed by author, January 2003. Murray Gunn in Alwyn Owen and Jack Perkins, *Speaking for Ourselves: Echoes from New Zealand's past, from the award-winning 'Spectrum' radio series*, Penguin Books, 1986, p. 27.
28. Brian Swete, written comm., 14 June 1993.
29. Doug Gunn, interviewed by author, 28 August 2004.
30. Derek Turnbull, interviewed by author, 4 April 1994.
31. Sharpe, *Fiordland Muster*, p. 103.
32. Arthur Bradshaw, *Flying by Bradshaw: Memoirs of a pioneer pilot 1933–1975*, ed. D. Phillips and G. McConnell, Proctor Publications, 2000, p. 67.
33. Brian Swete, interviewed by Jennifer Beveridge, 2 January 2005.
34. Doug Gunn, interviewed by author, 8 July 2005.
35. Ian Speden, interviewed by author, 11 July 2005.
36. Jill Collier, preface to Donaldson-Law, *Hollyford Muster 1948*, p. 9.
37. Donaldson-Law, *Hollyford Muster 1948*, p. 22.
38. Ibid., p. 47.
39. Sharpe, *Fiordland Muster*, pp. 20, 25. Derek Turnbull, interviewed by author, 4 May 1994. Prust, 'Gunn of the Hollyford', p. 30. Gordon Speden, obituary for David John Gunn, Gordon Speden Collection.
40. Ray Wilson, interviewed by Jack Perkins, c.1990, op. cit.
41. Ian Speden, interviewed by author, 19 March 2004.
42. Ian Haggitt, interviewed by author, 26 April 1994. David John Gunn to Dorothy Gunn, 5 July 1947, 12 August 1947, Murray Gunn Collection.
43. Elisabeth Stuart-Jones, *Hollyford Valley Track, December 1951*, Murray Gunn Collection. Elisabeth Stuart-Jones, pers. comm., 2 October 2005.
44. Lesley Board, pers. comm., 8 September 2005.
45. Doug Gunn, interviewed by author, 28 August 2004.
46. Prust, 'Gunn of the Hollyford', p. 4.
47. Murray Gunn, interviewed by author, January 2003.
48. Derek Turnbull, interviewed by author, 4 May 1994. Prust, 'Gunn of the Hollyford', p. 5.
49. Brian Scott, 'Notes on "Gunn's Camp", Hollyford', Misc-MS-0873, Hocken Library, Dunedin.
50. Arnold Grey, interviewed by author, 23 February 1993.
51. Murray Gunn, interviewed by author, January 2003.
52. Ibid. Isabel Findlay in *Southland Times*, 22 May 1999.
53. Isabel Findlay, interviewed by author, 1 September 2004.
54. Murray Gunn, written comm. to author, April 2003.
55. Dorothy Parlane, written comm. to author, December 2003.
56. Isabel Findlay, interviewed by author, January 2005.
57. Jill Collier, preface to Donaldson-Law, *Hollyford Muster*, p. 9.
58. Isabel Findlay, interviewed by author, 1 September 2004.
59. Murray Gunn, interviewed by author, January 2003.

Chapter Four

1. *Southland Times*, 2 January 1937
2. G. G. Stewart, 'A Wilderness of Enchantment: South Westland and beyond', *New Zealand Railways Magazine*, 1 March 1937. Inquest report, Walter Sutton Jones, J46 1937/551, Archives NZ, Wellington.
3. Arthur Bradshaw, *Flying by Bradshaw: Memoirs of a pioneer pilot 1933–1975*, ed. David Phillips and Graeme McConnell, Proctor Publications, 2000, p. 37. *Southland Times*, 2 January 1937. R. J. Cuthill, 'Heroic Trek', *Southland Times*, 11 June 1994.

4. Inquest evidence, *Southland Times*, 3 May 1937. Bradshaw, *Flying by Bradshaw*, p. 37.

5. Inquest evidence by Gunn, Bradshaw, passengers and Robbie, *Southland Times*, 3 May 1937. Bradshaw, ibid., p. 38. Cuthill, 'Heroic Trek', gives an overview of the differing versions of the story.

6. Bradshaw, ibid., p. 38.

7. *Southland Times*, 9 April 1937. Cuthill, 'Heroic Trek'. Bradshaw, ibid., pp. 37–40.

8. Elsie K. Morton, *Otago Daily Times*, 20 January 1962, p. 9.

9. Murray Gunn, interviewed by author, January 2003.

10. Stewart, 'South Westland and Beyond'.

11. Morton, *Otago Daily Times*, 20 January 1962, p. 9.

12. *Southland Times*, 2 January 1937.

13. Bradshaw, *Flying by Bradshaw*, p. 38.

14. *Southland Times*, 2 January 1937.

15. Ibid.

16. Stewart, 'South Westland and Beyond'. Morton, *Otago Daily Times*. Ian Speden, interviewed by author, 19 March 2004.

17. *Southland Times*, 15 January 1837.

18. *Southland Times*, 19, 20, 21, 22, 23, 25, 26, 27, 28, 30 January 1937; 1, 2, 4, 8 February 1937; 23 March 1937.

19. Cuthill, 'Heroic Trek'.

20. Ibid.

21. *Southland Times*, 12 May 1937. Murray Gunn, phone conversation with author, 3 March 2006.

22. 'Courage of Nurse Robbie', *Southland Times*, 9 April 1937. Cuthill, 'Heroic Trek'. Index of Probates, Archives NZ, Christchurch. Bradshaw, *Flying by Bradshaw*. *Wanganui Chronicle*, 27 June 1989.

23. Gordon Donaldson-Law, *Hollyford Muster 1948*, Sylvia Donaldson-Law, Nelson, 1995, p. 32. Davey's annual profit was probably between £100 and £200. Doug Gunn, interviewed by author, 28 August 2004.

24. *Southland Times*, 19, 20, 21, 22, 23, 25, 26, 27, 28, 30 January 1937; 1, 2, 4, 8 February 1937.

Chapter Five

1. Olga Sansom, 'Davey Gunn of the Hollyford', *New Zealand Listener*, 11 September 1959, p. 5.

2. For example: Eric James, 'Exploration in Unknown Otago: Part 1: The journey to Martins Bay', *Otago Daily Times*, c.21 August 1930. Alex Dickie, 'From the Hollyford to the Arawata', *New Zealand Alpine Journal*, 1934, Vol. 5, pp. 307–22. G. G. Stewart, 'A Wilderness of Enchantment: South Westland and beyond', *New Zealand Railways Magazine*, 1 March 1937. Alice Mackenzie, 'Early Struggles at Martins Bay', *Southland Times*, 8 September 1938.

3. Jean Prust, 'Gunn of the Hollyford', unpub. manuscript, copies held by Julia Bradshaw, Murray Gunn and Hocken Library (Barlow Papers, MS-1416/103) but original not located, p. 16.

4. Sansom, 'Davey Gunn of the Hollyford', p. 5.

5. Peter Newton, *Sixty Thousand on the Hoof*, A. H. & A. W. Reed, Wellington, 1975, p. 220.

6. Gordon Donaldson-Law, *Hollyford Muster 1948*, Sylvia Donaldson-Law, Nelson, 1995, p. 27.

7. Prust, 'Gunn of the Hollyford', p. 13.

8. Ibid., pp. 13–16.

9. Derek Turnbull, interviewed by author, 4 May 1994.

10. Prust, 'Gunn of the Hollyford', pp. 13–14.

11. Murray Gunn, written comm. to author, 4 August 2003.

12. Rupert Sharpe, *Fiordland Muster*, Hodder and Stoughton, London, 1966, p. 25.

13. Derek Turnbull, interviewed by author, 4 May 1994.

14. Prust, 'Gunn of the Hollyford', p. 14.

15. Sharpe, *Fiordland Muster*, pp. 57–59.

16. Derek Turnbull, interviewed by author, 4 May 1994.

17. Ed Cotter, interviewed by author, 2 December 1992.

18. Quoted by Sharpe, *Fiordland Muster*, p. 60.

19. Prust, 'Gunn of the Hollyford', pp. 19–20.

20. Murray Gunn, undated written comm. to author. Sharpe, *Fiordland Muster*, p. 55.

21. Ed Cotter, interviewed by author, 2 December 1992.

22. Sharpe, *Fiordland Muster*, pp. 76–78.

23. Donaldson-Law, *Hollyford Muster*, p. 28.

24. Ibid., p. 30.

25. Ed Cotter, interviewed by author, 2 December 1992.

26. Donaldson-Law, *Hollyford Muster*, p. 33.

27. Donaldson-Law, *Hollyford Muster*, p. 35.

28. Ed Cotter, interviewed by author, 2 December 1992.

29. Prust, 'Gunn of the Hollyford', p. 21.

30. Jim Speden quoted by Rupert Sharpe writing under his pen-name, 'Wanderer', in *New Zealand Free Lance*, 7 December 1949, p. 38.

31. Prust, 'Gunn of the Hollyford', p. 22.

32. Elfin McDonald, written comm. to author, November 2004.

33. Prust, 'Gunn of the Hollyford', p. 22.

34. 'Wanderer', *New Zealand Free Lance*.

35. Ed Cotter, interviewed by author, 2 December 1992.

36. Prust, 'Gunn of the Hollyford', p. 23.

37. Murray Gunn, interviewed by author, January 2003.

38. Prust, 'Gunn of the Hollyford', p. 24.

39. Derek Turnbull, interviewed by author, 4 May 1994.

Chapter Six

1. George Shaw's comment to Brian Swete, written comm. to author, 14 June 1993. Murray Gunn (interviewed by author, January 2003) reiterated this.
2. Arnold Grey, interviewed by author, 23 February 1993. Jean Prust, 'Gunn of the Hollyford', unpub. manuscript, copies held by Julia Bradshaw, Murray Gunn and Hocken Library (Barlow Papers, MS-1416/103) but original not located, p. 24. Murray Gunn, interviewed by author, 24 December 2005.
3. Murray Gunn, interviewed by author, 24 December 2005. Rupert Sharpe, *Fiordland Muster*, Hodder and Stoughton, London, 1966, p. 127. Prust, 'Gunn of the Hollyford', p. 24. Gordon Donaldson-Law, *Hollyford Muster 1948*, Sylvia Donaldson-Law, Nelson, 1995, p. 24.
4. Donaldson-Law, *Hollyford Muster 1948*, p. 21.
5. Arnold Grey, interviewed by author, 23 February 1993.
6. Ed Cotter, interviewed by author, 2 December 1992.
7. Prust, 'Gunn of the Hollyford' p. 26. Ian Haggitt, interviewed by author, 25 April 1994.
8. Prust, 'Gunn of the Hollyford', p. 24. Donaldson-Law, *Hollyford Muster*, p. 35.
9. Sharpe, *Fiordland Muster*, p. 26.
10. Prust, 'Gunn of the Hollyford', p. 26.
11. Brian Swete, interviewed by Jennifer Beveridge, 2 January 2005.
12. Murray Gunn, written comm. to author, September 2003.
13. Gerald Henry Hamilton, 'The Amateur Cowboy', *Wide World Magazine*, probably May 1947 although original not located, reproduced in Donaldson-Law, *Hollyford Muster*, p. 10.
14. Alan Snook, phone conversation with author, 25 September 2005.
15. Ibid.
16. Ibid.
17. Ibid.
18. Murray Gunn, written comm. to author, 4 August 2003. Daphne Midgley, interviewed by author, 8 July 2005.
19. Sharpe, *Fiordland Muster*, p. 68.
20. Derek Turnbull, interviewed by author, 4 May 1994.
21. *Stones Otago/Southland Directory, 1936–1945*.
22. Bill Brown, phone conversation with author, 3 March 2006.
23. *75 Years Service: A review of Campbell Park School 1908–1983*, published by P. G. Aspen, 1983, p. 7. Ian Speden, written comm. to author, 31 October 2005.
24. Ian Speden, interviewed by author, 11 July 2005. Daphne Midgley, interviewed by author, 8 July 2005.
25. Alan Snook, phone conversation with author, 25 September 2005.
26. Derek Turnbull, interviewed by author, 4 May 1994. Alan Snook, phone conversation with author, 25 September 2005.
27. Alan Snook, phone conversation with author, 25 September 2005.
28. Inquest report, J46, 142/1943, Murtagh, Archives NZ, Wellington.
29. Ibid.
30. Doug Gunn, interviewed by author, 28 August 2004. Murray Gunn, written comm. to author, April 2003.
31. For example: Alex Dickie, 'From the Hollyford to the Arawata', *New Zealand Alpine Journal*, 1934, Vol. 5, pp. 307–22. *Southland Times* (6 February 1943, p. 4), reporting Murtagh's death, concluded the article with two paragraphs about the Big Bay rescue.

Chapter Seven

1. Davey Gunn quoted in *Southland News*, 28 October 1950.
2. Isabel Findlay, interviewed by author, 1 September 2004 (confirmed by Doug Gunn). Dunedin District Manager to General Manager, Department of Tourist and Health Resorts, Wellington, 30 October 1926, file: Track Hollyford/Routeburn 1914–1939, TO 1, 38/51, part 3, Archives NZ, Wellington.
3. Dunedin District Manager to General Manager, Department of Tourist and Health Resorts, Wellington, 29 September 1927, file: ibid. Gordon Speden, obituary for David John Gunn, Gordon Speden Collection. Gus Tapper to Gordon Speden, 11 September 1933, with notes by Gordon Speden, Gordon Speden Collection.
4. A. & W. Hamilton to Minister in Charge of Tourist Resorts, 16 January 1935, and Invercargill District Manager to General Manager, 21 July 1936, file: ibid. 'More Visitors Make Trip to Hollyford', *Southland News*, 28 October 1950.
5. A. & W. Hamilton to General Manager, Tourist Department, 16 May 1938, file: ibid.
6. Murray Gunn, interviewed by author, January 2003.
7. A. & W. Hamilton, *See the Best of Southland*, brochure, c.1937, Murray Gunn Collection.
8. A. & W. Hamilton's description of the huts they managed in the Fiordland district, file: Track Hollyford/Routeburn 1914–1939, op. cit.
9. *Hollyford, Martins Bay, Big Bay and Pyke Walking*

and Riding Round Trip, brochure, c.1949, Tourist Department file: Te Anau Lake Wakatipu Track, TO 38/51, part 4, Archives NZ, Wellington.

10. Patience Lang, 'A Hollyford Holiday', 1955, Murray Gunn Collection. Ed Cotter, interviewed by author 2 December 1992.

11. Gordon Donaldson-Law, *Hollyford Muster 1948*, Sylvia Donaldson-Law, Nelson, 1995, p. 18.

12. 'M.A.S.', 'Meanderings in our Mountains' *Otago Daily Times*, 9 April 1938. A. & W. Hamilton to General Manager, Tourist Department, 16 May 1938, file: Track Hollyford/Routeburn 1914–1939, op. cit. G. G. Stewart, 'South Westland and Beyond', *New Zealand Railways Magazine*, 1 March 1937, pp. 15–16.

13. 'D. Le H. M.', 'Riding Down the Lower Hollyford', *Outdoors* (Otago Tramping Club magazine), June 1937, Vol. 3, No. 4.

14. John Hall Jones, *Martins Bay*, Craig Printing, 1988, p. 89.

15. 'I. S.', 'A Trip to the Lower Hollyford', *Outdoors*, June 1938, Vol. 4, No. 4, pp. 2–5.

16. 'D. Le H. M.', 'Riding Down the Lower Hollyford'.

17. Arnold Grey, interviewed by author, 23 February 1993.

18. Margaret McClure, *The Wonder Country: Making New Zealand tourism*, Auckland University Press, 2004, pp. 161–62.

19. Derek Turnbull, interviewed by author, 4 May 1994. Davey's 1955 brochure, NZ Forest Service file, F1 W3129, 38/7/25/1, box 245, Archives NZ, Wellington.

20. Gerald Henry Hamilton, 'The Amateur Cowboy', *Wide World Magazine*, May 1947, in Donaldson-Law, *Hollyford Muster*, p. 10.

21. Brian Swete, interviewed by his daughter Jennifer Beveridge, 2 January 2005. Doug Gunn interviewed by author 28 August 2004. Ian Speden, interviewed by author, 19 March 2004.

22. Doug Gunn, interviewed by author, 28 August 2004. Hamilton, 'The Amateur Cowboy', p. 10.

23. Promotional letter from David Gunn and Gerald H. Hamilton, 22 September 1945, Murray Gunn Collection.

24. Ibid.

25. 'More Visitors Make Trip to Hollyford', *Southland News*, 28 October 1950.

26. Elisabeth Stuart-Jones, *Diary of Hollyford Valley Walk, December 1951*, Murray Gunn Collection.

27. Ed Cotter, interviewed by author, 2 December 1992.

28. Rupert Sharpe, *Fiordland Muster*, Hodder and Stoughton, London, 1966, p. 38.

29. F. J. Lucas, *Popeye Lucas, Queenstown*, A. H. & A. W. Reed, Wellington, 1968, p. 125.

30. Ed Cotter, interviewed by author, 2 December 1992.

31. Ibid.

32. Lang, 'A Hollyford Holiday'.

33. Ibid.

34. Gordon Speden to Bert Cocks of Te Hapa Kura Tramping Club, 3 February 1947, Gordon Speden Collection.

35. Doug Gunn, interviewed by author, 28 August 2004.

36. Ibid. Ian Speden, interviewed by author, 19 March 2004.

37. Olga Sansom, 'Davey Gunn of the Hollyford', *NZ Listener*, 11 September 1959, p. 5.

38. Peter Newton, *Sixty Thousand on the Hoof*, A. H. & A. W. Reed, Wellington, 1975, pp. 226–27.

39. Gerald H. Hamilton to Mr Swift, 20 May 1946, Tourist Department file: Te Anau Lake Wakatipu Track, op. cit.

40. Correspondence in Tourist Department file: ibid.

41. Hall Jones, *Martins Bay*, pp. 132–33. Letters from T. L. Macdonald, 13, 18 August 1947, Tourist Department file: ibid. Gordon Speden, interviewed by Geoff Spearpoint, 30 March 1983.

42. Gordon Speden, interviewed by Geoff Spearpoint, 30 March 1983.

43. Letter from T. L. Macdonald, 18 August 1947, Tourist Department file: Te Anau Lake Wakatipu Track, op. cit.

44. Public Works Department Engineer's report, 3 November 1947, and letters from T. L. Macdonald, 18 August 1947 and 21 February 1948, file: ibid.

45. Letter from T. L. Macdonald, 18 August 1947, Tourist Department file: ibid.

46. Public Works Department Engineer's report, 3 November 1947; Parry to Macdonald, 18 March 1948; PWD to Department of Tourist and Health Resorts, 20 January 1948, Tourist Department file: ibid.

47. Resident Engineer in Invercargill to Under-Secretary PWD, 20 April 1948, Tourist Department file: ibid.

48. T. L. Macdonald to Gordon Speden, 4 July 1948, Gordon Speden Collection. Jean Prust, 'Gunn of the Hollyford', unpub. manuscript, copies held by Julia Bradshaw, Murray Gunn and Hocken Library (Barlow Papers, MS-1416/103) but original not located, pp. 34–36.

49. Prust, 'Gunn of the Hollyford', pp. 34–36.

50. Ibid.

51. Arnold Grey, interviewed by author, 23 February 1993. Ian Speden, interviewed by author, 19 March 2004.
52. Murray Gunn, interviewed by author, January 2003. Newton, *Sixty Thousand*, pp. 226–27.
53. Doug Gunn, interviewed by author, 28 August 2004.

Chapter Eight

1. Licence M345 for 2,000 acres in the Hollyford Valley, file: DAFU/D311/168q-M345, Archives NZ, Dunedin.
2. Murray Gunn, interviewed by author, January 2003. Arnold Grey, interviewed by author, 23 February 1993. Jean Prust, 'Gunn of the Hollyford', unpub. manuscript, copies held by Julia Bradshaw, Murray Gunn and Hocken Library (Barlow Papers, MS-1416/103) but original not located, p. 3.
3. Runs Register, c.1878–c.1960, file: DAAK D84 768, Archives NZ, Dunedin. Alteration plate, December 1949, file: DAFU/D311 168q-M345, Archives NZ, Dunedin.
4. *Southland Daily News*, 15 September 1950. Prust, 'Gunn of the Hollyford', pp. 29–31.
5. *Southland Daily News*, 15 September 1950.
6. Ibid.
7. Prust, 'Gunn of the Hollyford', p. 30. Ray Wilson, interviewed by Jack Perkins, c.1990, 97/120 BC92/34, Sound Archives Nga Taonga Korero, Christchurch.
8. *Southland Daily News*, 15 September 1950.
9. Ibid. Jim Speden quoted by Prust, 'Gunn of the Hollyford', p. 31. Murray Gunn, pers. comm., 31 March 2004.
10. Anon. but probably written by F. W. G. Miller, reproduced in Prust, 'Gunn of the Hollyford', p. 29, but not acknowledged (it is believed it originally appeared in the *Southland Daily News*).
11. Murray Gunn, interviewed by author, January 2003. Prust, 'Gunn of the Hollyford', p. 31
12. Prust, 'Gunn of the Hollyford', p. 31.
13. Murray Gunn, interviewed by author, January 2003.
14. Probate, Isabella Grierson Gunn, file: CH145 TU 7395/1951, Archives NZ, Christchurch.
15. Probate, Alexander Gunn, file: CH145 TU 1982/1922, Archives NZ, Christchurch.
16. 'More Visitors Make Trip to Hollyford', *Southland Daily News*, 28 October 1950. Gordon Speden, interviewed by Geoff Spearpoint, 30 March 1983. Brian Scott, 'Notes on "Gunn's Camp", Hollyford', Misc-MS-0873, Hocken Library, Dunedin.
17. Scott, 'Notes on "Gunn's Camp", Hollyford'. Doug Gunn, interviewed by author, 28 August 2004.
18. Elisabeth Stuart-Jones, *Diary of Hollyford Valley Walk, December 1951*, Murray Gunn Collection.
19. Gordon Speden, interviewed by Geoff Spearpoint, 30 March 1983.
20. Jean Prust, interviewed by author, 1 December 1992. Murray Gunn, interviewed by author, January 2003. Death certificate for Alice Jean Prust, 1995/1796, Registrar of Births, Deaths & Marriages, Lower Hutt.
21. Doug Gunn, interviewed by author, 28 August 2004. Brian Swete, interviewed by Jennifer Beveridge, 2 January 2005.
22. For example, Ian Speden, Doug Gunn, Daphne Midgley. Ed Cotter, interviewed by author, 2 December 1992.
23. Murray Gunn, interviewed by author, January 2003.
24. Ibid.
25. Daphne Midgley, interviewed by author, 8 July 2005.
26. Doug Gunn, interviewed by author, 8 July 2005.
27. Ibid.
28. Probate, David John Gunn, DAFG/9064/157:270/56, Archives NZ, Dunedin.
29. Doug Gunn, interviewed by author, 28 August 2004.
30. *Dominion*, 9 January 1952 and 10 January 1952, p. 8.
31. *Evening Post*, 9 January 1952, p. 8. Information for the following account was from file: Inquest Algie/Williams, file: J46 861/1952, Archives NZ, Wellington; Doug Gunn, interviewed by author, 28 August 2004; *Evening Post*, 9 January 1952, p. 8; *Dominion*, 10 January 1952, p. 8; miscellaneous undated newspaper clippings courtesy of Ian Robertson, now in author's collection.
32. Dan McKenzie in an unsourced newspaper clipping, c.1952, courtesy of Ian Robertson, now in author's collection.
33. Miscellaneous undated newspaper clippings, courtesy of Ian Robertson, now in author's collection.
34. Doug Gunn, interviewed by author, 28 August 2004.
35. Newspaper clippings, courtesy of Ian Robertson, now in author's collection.
36. Inquest record: J46 861/1952, Algie and Williams, Archives NZ, Wellington. *Southland Times*, 23 July 1952, pp. 6, 8. Murray Gunn, pers. comm.
37. Southern Scenic Air Services Ltd to Commissioner of Crown Lands, 5 November 1953, file: DAFU/D324/47a/4/20, Archives NZ, Dunedin. Lakes County Council Rates Books, Lakes District Museum, Arrowtown.
38. Williams (Assistant Forester Tuatapere) to Conservator

of Forests Invercargill, 23 March 1953, file: Hollyford & Pyke Forest 1953–67, CAMP/D23/86r 6/7/25 State Forest No. 25, Archives NZ, Dunedin.

39. Mrs Peter Mackenzie (formerly Alice McKenzie of Martins Bay), *Pioneers of Martins Bay*, Otago Daily Times and Witness Newspapers Co. Ltd, 1947.

40. Murray Gunn, interviewed by author, January 2003.

41. Brian Swete, phone conversation with author, 4 May 2005.

42. Brian Swete, written comm. to author, 14 June 1993.

43. John Hall Jones, *Martins Bay*, Craig Printing, 1988, p. 90.

44. 'Airstrip Being Built at Martins Bay', *Evening Star*, 26 February 1953, p. 3.

45. This figure is quoted in a report by P. K. Dorizac, park ranger, 31 October 1957, file: DAFU/D324/135g/13/1/34, Archives NZ, Dunedin.

46. Ed Cotter, interviewed by author, 2 December 1992.

47. Brian Swete, phone conversation with author, 4 May 2005. Brian Swete, written comm. to author, 14 June 1993.

48. Murray Gunn, interviewed by author, January 2003.

49. Report by Dorizac, park ranger, 31 October 1957, op. cit. Brian Swete, interviewed by Jennifer Beveridge, 2 January 2005.

Chapter Nine

1. Murray Gunn, interviewed by author, January 2003.

2. Jean Prust, 'Gunn of the Hollyford', unpublished manuscript, copies held by Julia Bradshaw, Murray Gunn and Hocken Library (Barlow Papers, MS-1416/103) but original not located, p. 7.

3. Murray Gunn, interviewed by author, January 2003.

4. Doug Gunn, interviewed by author, 28 August 2004. Rupert Sharpe, *Fiordland Muster*, Hodder and Stoughton, London, 1966, p. 67. Murray Gunn, undated written comm. to author. Inspection of Forests in Hollyford and Pyke Valleys, 10 March 1953, file: Hollyford & Pyke Forest, 1953–67, CAMP/D23/86r, 6/7/25, State Forest No. 25, Archives NZ, Dunedin.

5. Inspection of Forests in Hollyford and Pyke Valleys, ibid.

6. Lands & Survey Department report on Runs 471 to 474, 14 January 1954, file: DAFU/D324/47a/4/20, Archives NZ, Dunedin.

7. Ibid.

8. Case No. 151, National Parks Authority meeting, 6 December 1954, copy from Murray Gunn Collection, original not located but copy is stamped

'National Archives of New Zealand, Head Office, Wellington'.

9. Lands & Survey Department report on Runs 471 to 474, op. cit.

10. Murray Gunn, interviewed by author, January 2003.

11. Case No. 151, op. cit.

12. Ibid.

13. Lands & Survey Department report on Runs 471 to 474, op. cit.

14. Many people commented on this, for example Patience Lang, 'A Hollyford Holiday, February 1955' (Murray Gunn Collection), and rangers L. W. Hinchey and K. M. Wright, January 1954, DAFU/D324/47a/4/20, Archives NZ, Dunedin.

15. Eoin Wylie, interviewed by author, 18 June 1992.

16. Ibid.

17. Murray Gunn, interviewed by Morag Forrester, 15–17 June 1998.

18. Murray Gunn, interviewed by author, January 2003.

19. Murray Gunn, interviewed by Morag Forrester, 31 May 2000.

20. Ibid.

21. Gordon Speden, interviewed by Geoff Spearpoint, 30 March 1983. Prust, 'Gunn of the Hollyford', p. 40.

22. Ed Cotter, interviewed by author, May 2006. Murray Gunn, interviewed by author, January 2003. Murray Gunn to Gordon and Emma Speden, 7 June 1955, Gordon Speden Collection.

23. Ed Cotter, interviewed by author, May 2006. Murray Gunn, interviewed by author, January 2003. Murray Gunn, written comm. to author, 3 December 2005.

24. Murray Gunn, interviewed by author, January 2003.

25. *Otago Daily Times*, 30 December 1955, p. 1. Prust, 'Gunn of the Hollyford', p. 38. Inquest report, D. J. Gunn, file: J46 1956/594, Archives NZ, Wellington.

26. Dorothy Andrews, pers. comm., 12 June 2006. Prust, 'Gunn of the Hollyford', p. 39. Inquest report, ibid.

27. Murray Gunn, interviewed by author, January 2003. Brian Swete, phone conversation with author, 4 May 2005.

28. Ibid.

29. Murray Gunn, interviewed by author, 24 December 2005. Isabel Findlay, interviewed by author, 1 September 2004.

30. Inquest report, op. cit.

31. Ibid. Murray Gunn, interviewed by author, 24 December 2005. George Burnby, interviewed by author, April 2003.

32. Murray Gunn, interviewed by author, January 2003.

Chapter Ten

1. Dusty Spittle, lyric from 'Old Davey Gunn', reproduced with permission.
2. Gordon Speden Collection.
3. Not dated but all January 1956, Murray Gunn Collection.
4. *Otago Daily Times*, 31 December 1955, p. 1. Inquest report, D. J. Gunn, file: J46 1956/594, Archives NZ, Wellington.
5. NZ Forest Service File: F1 W3129 38/7/25/1, box 245, Archives NZ, Wellington.
6. Public Trust Office to the Commissioner of Crown Lands, 28 February 1956, file: DAFU/D311/68q-M345, Archives NZ, Dunedin
7. Ibid.
8. Daphne Midgley, interviewed by author, 8 July 2005. Derek and Pat Turnbull, interviewed by author, Easter 2004.
9. Jean Prust, 'Gunn of the Hollyford', unpub. manuscript, copies held by Julia Bradshaw, Murray Gunn and Hocken Library (Barlow Papers, MS-1416/103) but original not located, p. 38.
10. NZ Forest Service file, op. cit. Murray Gunn to Director-General of Lands, 11 December 1957, file: DAFU/D324/135g 13/1/34, Archives NZ, Dunedin.
11. Commissioner of Crown Lands, 21 May 1958, file: DAFU/D311 168q-M345, Archives NZ, Dunedin.
12. Ruth Waddell, interviewed by author, 1 May 1994.
13. Hut book from Martins Bay whitebaiter's hut, entry by W. H. Evans, H. K. Dukes and A. J. W. Campbell, 12–22 February 1959, courtesy of Neil Drysdale.
14. Elsie K. Morton, two articles in unnamed newspapers, Murray Gunn Collection. Brian and Ruth Waddell, interviewed by author, 1 May 1994.
15. Park ranger Dorizac to Fiordland National Park Board, 26 October 1959, file: F1 W3129 38/7/25/1, box 245, Archives NZ, Wellington.
16. Director-General NZ Forest Service to Minister of Forests, 5 January 1966, file: ibid.
17. Eoin Wylie, interviewed by author, 18 June 1992.
18. Ibid.
19. Unsourced newspaper clipping, Murray Gunn Collection. Eoin Wylie, interviewed by author, 18 June 1992.
20. Fiordland National Park Board, 29 March 1966, file: F1 W3129 38/7/25/1, Archives NZ, Wellington.
21. File: ABWN 6095 W5021 458, record 16/2982, part 1, Archives NZ, Wellington. NZ Forest Service File, op. cit.
22. NZ Forest Service File, ibid. Adventours brochure, Gordon Speden Collection. Ed Cotter, interviewed by author, May 2006.
23. NZ Forest Service File, op. cit. Hollyford Tourist & Travel Co. Ltd brochure, c. 1970. Morag Forrester, Hollyford Track research for Department of Conservation, 2006.
24. *Otago Daily Times*, 20 January 1962, p. 9; 18 December 1965, p. 13. *Evening Star*, 28 June 1962, p. 18.
25. Death certificate for Alice Jean Prust, 1995/1796, Registrar of Births, Deaths & Marriages, Lower Hutt.
26. Brian Swete, written comm. with author, 14 June 1993.
27. Marriage registration for Ruth Benstead, 1960/15678, Registrar or Births, Deaths & Marriages, Lower Hutt. Murray Gunn, interviewed by author, 24 December 2005.
28. *Southland Times*, 22 May 1999.
29. Rupert Sharpe, *Fiordland Muster*, Hodder and Stoughton, London, 1966.
30. Gordon Donaldson-Law, *Hollyford Muster 1948*, Sylvia D. Donaldson-Law, 1995.
31. Prust, 'Gunn of the Hollyford'.
32. Dusty Spittle, phone conversation with author, 3 November 2006.
33. Joe Charles in Les Cleveland, *The Great New Zealand Songbook*, Godwit Press, Auckland 1995, pp. 60–61.
34. Elisabeth Stuart-Jones, 'Hollyford Valley Track, December 1951', Murray Gunn Collection.

Bibliography

Official records

Appendix to the Journals of the House of Representatives (AJHR), Sheep owners' returns, H–23b, 1918–1926

Births, Deaths and Marriages Records, Central Registry, Lower Hutt

Department of Conservation, Southland Conservancy files, Archives NZ/Te Rua Mahara o te Kawanatanga, Dunedin

Department of Justice, Lands & Deeds Registry Office files, Archives NZ/Te Rua Mahara o te Kawanatanga, Dunedin

Department of Lands and Survey files, Archives NZ/Te Rua Mahara o te Kawanatanga, Dunedin and Wellington

Intention to Marry records, Archives NZ/Te Rua Mahara o te Kawanatanga, Wellington

Land Information New Zealand, Dunedin Regional Office files, Archives NZ/Te Rua Mahara o te Kawanatanga, Dunedin

Marine Department, Series 1, Archives NZ/Te Rua o te Kawanatanga, Wellington

New Zealand Defence Force, Personnel Archives, Archives NZ/Te Rua Mahara o te Kawanatanga, Wellington

New Zealand electoral rolls

New Zealand Forest Service, Series 1, Archives NZ/Te Rua Mahara o te Kawanatanga, Wellington

New Zealand Forest Service, Tuatapere office files, Archives NZ/Te Rua Mahara o te Kawanatanga, Dunedin

New Zealand Yearbook 1936, Government Printer, Wellington, 1935

Probate files, Archives NZ/Te Rua Mahara o te Kawanatanga, Wellington, Christchurch, Dunedin

Tourist and Publicity Department, Series 1, Archives NZ/Te Rua Mahara o te Kawanatanga, Wellington

Published sources

75 Years Service: A review of Campbell Park School 1908–1983, published by P. G. Aspen, Oamaru, 1983

Anderson, Harold J., *Men of the Milford Road*, 2nd edn, Craig Printing Co., Invercargill, 1985

Anderson, W. A., *Doctor in the Mountains*, A. H. & A. W. Reed, Wellington, 1967

Beattie, W. B., *Bill Beattie's New Zealand*, Hodder & Stoughton, Auckland, 1970

Bradshaw, Arthur, *Flying by Bradshaw: Memoirs of a pioneer pilot 1933–1975*, ed. David Phillips and Graeme McConnell, Proctor Publications, 2000

Charles, Joe, *Black Billy Tea: New Zealand Ballads*, Whitcoulls, Wellington, 1981

Cleveland, Les, *The Great New Zealand Songbook*, Godwit Press, Auckland, 1991

Donaldson-Law, Gordon, *Hollyford Muster 1948,* Sylvia Donaldson-Law, Nelson, 1995

Hall Jones, John, *Martins Bay*, Craig Printing Co., Invercargill, 1988

Hooker, R. H., *The Archaeology of South Westland Maori*, New Zealand Forest Service, Hokitika, 1986

Lucas, F. J., *Popeye Lucas, Queenstown*, A. H. & A. W. Reed, Wellington, 1968

Madgwick, Paul, *Aotea: A history of the South Westland Maori*, printed by Greymouth Evening Star, 1992

McAloon, Jim, *No Idle Rich: The wealthy in Canterbury & Otago 1840–1914*, Otago University Press, Dunedin, 2002

McClure, Margaret, *The Wonder Country: Making New Zealand tourism*, Auckland University Press, Auckland, 2004

Moir, George M., *Guide Book to the Tourist Routes of the Great Southern Lakes and Fiords of Western Otago*, 1925, ODT & Witness Newspapers Co.

Newton, Peter, *Sixty Thousand on the Hoof*, A. H. & A. W. Reed, Wellington, 1975

Owen, Alwyn and Jack Perkins, *Speaking for Ourselves: Echoes from New Zealand's past, from the award-winning 'Spectrum' radio series*, Penguin Books, Auckland, 1986

Parry, Gordon, *N.M.A. The story of the first 100 years: The National Mortgage and Agency Company of NZ Limited 1864–1964*, National Mortgage and Agency

Co. of New Zealand, Dunedin, 1964

Sharpe, Rupert, *Fiordland Muster*, Hodder and Stoughton, London, 1966

Stone's Otago/Southland Directory 1880–84, 1909, 1915–19, 1921, 1926, 1933–45

Thompson, H. M., *East of the Rock and Pillar: History of Strath Taieri and Macraes District*, Capper Press, 1977

Turner, Samuel, *Conquest of the Southern Alps*, Fisher & Unwin, London, 1922

Walton, J. H. (ed.), *Southland Tramper: 50th Jubilee Edition 1947–1997*, Southland Tramping Club, Invercargill, c.1998

White, Paula E., *The Baikies of Pike's Point, Glenavy, South Canterbury*, Waimate, 1993

Wise's New Zealand Directory, 1880–84, 1894, 1898

Personal communications and interviews

Andrews, Dot, written comm. to author, 12 June 2006

Board, Lesley, written comm. to author, 8 September 2005

Brown, Bill, phone conversation with author, 3 March 2006

Burnby, George, interviewed by author, April 2003

Cotter, Ed, interviewed by author, 2 December 1992, May 2006

De La Mare, Alan, interviewed by author, 1992

Findlay, Isabel, interviewed by author, 1 September 2004, 27 January 2005

Greenslade, Jean, interviewed by author, 30 January 1994

Grey, Arnold, interviewed by author, 23 February 1993

Gunn, Doug, interviewed by author, 28 August 2004, 8 July 2005

Gunn, Murray, interviewed by author, January 2003, 24 December 2005; interviewed by Morag Forrester, 15–17 June 1998, 31 May 2000; numerous written comms to author, 2003–06

Haggitt, Ian, interviewed by author, 26 April 1994

Jones, Kathryn Johan, interviewed by author, April 2004

Leaker, Margaret, written comm. to author, 31 August 2004

Marshall, Peter, written comm. to author, 14 June 2003

McDonald, Elfin, written comm. to author, November 2004

Midgley, Daphne, interviewed by author, 8 July 2005

Parlane, Dorothy, written comm. with author, December 2003

Snook, Alan, phone conversation with author, 25 September 2005

Speden, Gordon, interviewed by Geoff Spearpoint, 30 March 1983

Speden, Ian, interviewed by author, 19 March 2004,

11 July 2005; written comm. to author, 31 October 2005

Spittle, Dusty, phone conversation with author, 3 November 2006

Stuart Jones, Elisabeth, written comm. to author, 2 October 2005

Swete, Brian, written comm. to author, 14 June 1993; interviewed by Jennifer Beveridge, 2 January 2005; phone conversation with author, 4 May 2005

Thomson, Mary, written comm. to author, 16 March 2004

Turnbull, Derek, interviewed by author, 4 April 1994

Waddell, Brian and Ruth, interviewed by author, 1 May 1994

White, Paula written comm. to author, 22 June 2005

Wilson, Ray, interviewed by Jack Perkins, c.1990, 97/120, BC92/34, Sound Archives Archives Nga Taonga Korero, Christchurch

Wylie, Eoin, interviewed by author, 18 June 1992

Unpublished material and private papers

Gunn, Murray, collection of papers and photographs

Hakataramea Township School Records, North Otago Museum, Oamaru

Jones, Kathryn Johan, 'Gunn Family History', Murray Gunn Collection

Kroetsch, Laura C., 'Fine in the Morning: The life writing of Alice McKenzie', MA thesis, 1994, Victoria University of Wellington

Lake County Council rates books, Lakes District Museum, Arrowtown

Lang, Patience, 'A Hollyford Holiday, (February 1955)', Murray Gunn Collection

McCurdy, Lindsay, scrapbook, Mary Thompson, Waimate

McCurdy, Lindsay, accounts of trip in Hollyford, August 1934, Ann Irving, Invercargill

McDonald, David, diary, copy courtesy of the late David McDonald, Dunedin

Prust, Jean, 'Gunn of the Hollyford', unpublished manuscript, copies held by Julia Bradshaw, Murray Gunn and Hocken Collections, Uare Taoka o Hakena, University of Otago, (Barlow papers, MS-1416/103), but original not located

Scott, Brian, 'Notes on "Gunn's Camp", Hollyford', Misc-MS-0873, Hocken Collections/Uare Taoka o Hakena, University of Otago, Dunedin

Speden, Gordon, collection of papers and photographs, currently held by Ian Speden, to be donated to Hocken Collections/Uare Taoka o Hakena, University of Otago, Dunedin

Stuart-Jones, Elisabeth, 'Hollyford Valley Track,

December 1951', Murray Gunn Collection

Vance, W., papers, MS-Papers–111-11, Alexander Turnbull Library, Wellington

Waimate District rates records, Waimate District and Historical Society Archives

Waituna School roll, Waimate District and Historical Society Archives

Willetts, Freeman, 'The Willetts-Henderson Families', unpublished family history, Oamaru

Newspapers and periodicals

Dominion, Wellington

Evening Post, Wellington

Hokitika Guardian, Hokitika

Lake Wakatip Mail, Queenstown

New Zealand Alpine Journal, Dunedin

New Zealand Free Lance, Wellington

New Zealand Listener, Wellington

New Zealand Truth, Wellington

New Zealand Railways Magazine, Wellington

Oamaru Mail, Oamaru

Otago Daily Times, Dunedin

Outdoors, Dunedin

Southland Daily News, Invercargill

Southland Times, Invercargill

Tararua Tramper, Wellington

Wanganui Chronicle, Wanganui

West Coast Times, Hokitika

Wide World Magazine, London

Index